THE DAILY QUIET TIME

HERB HODGES

THE DAILY QUIET TIME

© 2013 Herb Hodges

ALL RIGHTS RESERVED

No part of this publication may be reproduced, stored in a retrieval system, or transmitted in any form without prior written permission.

Spiritual Life Ministries
2916 Old Elm Lane
Germantown, TN 38138
Herb Hodges – Executive Director

Web site: herbhodges.com
E-mail: herbslm@mindspring.com

Table of Contents

Introduction 5

Your Daily Quiet Time 7

The Matter of an Intimate
Relationship with God 25

Lessons to Carry to the Prayer Closet 31

Master Mottoes for Approaching God 37

Reading Prayer 43

Suggestions for Improving Your
Daily Quiet Time 49

The Priority of Prayer 55

The Christian Life and Prayer 77

The Master's Prayer 91

Prayer that Prevails 117

Remember – And Be Thankful 131

The Prayer of Jabez 157

Introduction

In this small book, we are going to look at one of the most indispensable themes or subjects in a believer's life: the matter of the individual's daily quiet time Or, as it has been called, your daily appointment with God. Others have called it the morning watch. It is simply the believer's daily devotional life, an absolutely indispensable aspect of spiritual life. In fact, the secret of a powerful Christian life launches in an individual's daily quiet time. The secret of a powerful Christian work launches both in the individual quiet time and in the corporate power represented by the corporate quiet times of all the Christian's involved. And, the secret of a powerful church is the same thing. They all launch from the individual's personal quiet time or daily devotional life with God.

The Secret of a Powerful Church

Some years ago, I was in a powerful little church and I had thought I had gone to lead the church in spiritual special services called revival. And I found to my amazement that I was actually there to be blessed more than I was to be a blessing. We had a number of people saved, we had lives changed, we had Christian's lives change, but most importantly was what happened to me. I saw a very, very, powerful small church where great miracles took place in service after service after service — the things that would be hard to explain from a mere human standpoint. Things that would require God as an explanation for. I was talking with the pastor one afternoon and he said "Would you like to see the primary secret?" And I said, "I sure would." And so that afternoon he took me over to a prayer service where two older Christian ladies were praying as they did every day. They had come out to that church when it had its first beginnings to help form its foundation and had remained. And they had discipled the people at large, the most of the people, in the matter of having a daily powerful quiet time.

In every home I entered that week I looked around upon cue:
- **a)** I found a small desk somewhere inside the door,
- **b)** I found a little stack of books on the corner of that desk,
- **c)** I found a Bible,
- **d)** I found a notebook that had a prayer list and devotional thoughts that were gleaned from the daily reading every day.

I was told that this was the secret of the power of the church, and my life became entirely changed. I had had something of a daily quiet time, but it became much more structured and much more powerful from that point on. And for over 40 years, with very few interruptions, I have had a quiet time essentially at the same time every morning with some interruptions because of schedule and other demands. And if not at that time, then usually some other time during the day, every day. And I can tell you that I do not believe a person can have a viable, vital Christian life without a daily quiet time. So I want to explore with you some aspects of the daily devotional life or what others have called "the morning watch."

My prayer for you is that these brief studies will so stir your heart that you will begin to make a divine appointment on a daily basis and cultivate a deepening fellowship with our Heavenly Father. And in so doing, you will glorify Him by enjoying Him. For as one pastor stated most concisely and eloquently: "God is most glorified in us when we are most satisfied in Him!

Chapter 1

YOUR DAILY QUIET TIME

Psalms 5:3: *"My voice shalt Thou hear in the morning, O Lord; in the morning will I direct my prayer unto Thee, and will look up."*

A man coming in from work one evening entered his home and found his wife sitting on the couch crying as if her heart was broken. He hurried over, sat down beside her, and inquired urgently, "Honey, what's wrong?" She tearfully replied, "I had it in my heart to be so good to you this evening, and everything has gone wrong!" I fixed all of your favorite dishes for dinner, and topped it off by fixing your very favorite big biscuits. But when I put the pan of biscuits out on the table to cool off, I made the mistake of leaving a chair out from the table. When I left the room, the dog jumped up on the chair, got on the table – and ate all of the biscuits!" And she began to cry uncontrollably again. Her husband slipped over to her side, put his arm around her, and said,

"There, there, honey, it's really nothing to cry about; *we can always get another dog!*"

You see, there are some things you can replace, and some things you cannot replace. There are some things that are absolutely necessary, and some things that are only relatively important. In this session, we want to look at one of the *absolutely important things in a Christian's life.* We want to look at his *daily quiet time.* Others have called it "the believer's morning watch." A military man wisely called it "the daily time in the Captain's briefing room." Whatever you may call it, your success as a Christian will rise and fall with your practice of the daily quiet time.

A deep-sea diver who is about to plunge into the depths of a very threatening environment would not think of going down into the water without first making sure that his air hose was connected so that he could get oxygen from above. What that air hose is to the diver, the daily quiet time is to the Christian. And a Christian should not enter into the activities, duties and temptations of the day (*any* day) without first making certain that his connections with heaven are clear and solid.

In this study, we will examine some of the vital dimensions of a daily quiet time.

I. The PRIORITY of the daily quiet time.

First, we will consider the *priority* of the daily quiet time. You always have time for the things that are most important to you. It is not really a question of time, but of values. The quiet time is more than a commendable practice; it is absolutely vital to a life of sustained spirituality, effectiveness and love. It is the barometer of the Christian life. Personally, I offer you little hope of living a life of victory in Christ unless you are successful in maintaining a daily quiet time.

II. The PLACE for it

Second, the *place* for the daily quiet time must be considered. Jesus spoke of this place as your prayer "closet" (Matt. 6:6). It should be, if possible, the most secluded, least cluttered, most comfortable, and most conducive spot in your setting. It should be well-lighted, and be furnished with at least a chair.

III. The PERIOD for it

The third important consideration is the *period* for the daily quiet time. When should we have it, and how much time should be devoted to it? The rule should be to "have enough time to forget time." Prayer is *a time exposure to God.* Prayer is to secure *our* adjustment to *God*, not to seek *God's* adjustment to *us*. An oarsman does not row the *shore* to the *boat*; he rows the *boat* to the *shore*.

George Muller, the great man of faith from Bristol, England, said, "A believer's first responsibility with each new day is to bring his own soul into a happy relationship before God." The goal should be to *seek God's face* each day before you *see* the face of any *man*. You are reserving the most strategic part of your day for this purpose. This is indeed your "briefing session in the Captain's Room." Everything else is vain without this.

The Biblical principle of first fruits should be observed here. When Israel went into the land of Canaan to conquer it, the first city taken was to be devoted to God in token of His ownership of the entire land. Following the same principle, the Biblical "rule" is that the first fruits of your substance, the first day of each week, and the first hour of each day should belong to God. "My voice shalt Thou hear in the morning, O Lord; in the morning will I direct my prayer unto Thee, and will look up" (Ps 5:3). "It's infinitely better to *pray* for help *early* than it is to *yell* for help *late*." Just as the manna was to be gathered in the morning, so should the treasures of the spiritual life be gathered in the morning.

We don't depend on the good meals we had last week or last year for our physical strength today. We must take time to eat every day to maintain strength and good health. You should determine right now that, just as you don't expect to spend a day between now and your death without food, so you will not spend a single day in this life without meeting with God for spiritual nourishment. No one can begin the day well, go on well, or end up well, who fails to make provision for this quiet time with God.

A cavalry officer in the Civil War was pursued by a large force of enemy soldiers. His soldiers back at the line kept urging him, "Hurry! They're gaining!" But the officer discovered that his saddle girth was loosening. Coolly the officer dismounted in the field, tightened the buckle on the saddle girth, then remounted and galloped to safety behind his line. The broken buckle would have left him on the field a prisoner. Stopping to repair the problem allowed him to go on amid the cheers of his army. The Christian who is in such a hurry that he neglects the time alone with God rides the battlefield with a broken buckle. Defeat and disaster are likely coming.

In a Spanish art gallery, there is a painting which shows a laborer ploughing a field with a plough attached to a yoke of oxen. He has completed half the field, but he has gotten into a fresh furrow and knelt on his knees. His eyes are closed, and his hands are folded in prayer. Back in the distant background may be seen the spire of a church, which apparently has rung out the call to prayer. But there is something the laborer doesn't know. As he is on his knees, an angel from heaven has descended from the skies, picked up his plough, has completed one row, and is turning the oxen to plough the next row. Under the picture there is this caption: **NO TIME LOST**. When a person takes time to meet with God, he does not lose time—*he gains eternity.*

IV. The PARAPHERNALIA (PARTS) of it

The fourth thing to consider is the *"parts"* of the daily quiet time. What materials should be used? Some materials are variable; others are indispensable. These materials are indispensable: at least two good translations of the Bible (New American Standard Version, Amplified Bible, New International Version, Living Bible paraphrase, Phillips paraphrase of the New Testament, and the King James Version are good possibilities to select from). Out of this list, I would prefer the NASV and the Amplified Bible, but I have used them all to advantage over the years. I strongly recommend that every Christian secure a copy of The Discovery Bible New Testament (NASV). This is an invaluable tool in studying the New Testament! Then, these additional materials should be used: a good daily devotional book (there are many; consult your pastor about a selection); a journal for notations; a prayer list; and a globe or manageable map of the world. Other materials are optional.

V. The PROCEDURE to follow

Fifth, let me suggest a possible *procedure* to follow. *Get quiet enough to switch from your normal active, aggressive mood into a passive, receptive mood.* Come before God with expectancy. Practice the "open hand" policy. First, open your hand and turn the palm *down*, picturing the *emptying* of your life. Then, turn the palm *up*, picturing your willingness to receive whatever God may want to give. Pause to be reminded of His Presence and His Promise (Heb. 13:5 & Ex. 34:2, as examples).

The Daily Quiet Time

Practice creative, focused silence. Be like King David, who "went in and sat before the Lord" (II Sam. 7:18).

> "Hold up your heart, dear child, for God to fill;
> He doesn't say, Be strong; He says, Be still."

Concentrate on Jesus. Begin with a brief prayer, such as Psalm 119:18, "Open Thou mine eyes, that I might behold wondrous things out of Thy Word." Remind yourself of the statement of Scripture in Psalm 119:130: "The entrance of Thy Word gives light; it gives understanding to the simple." Ask God to make you "simple" enough to receive His light during the time you spend with Him. Then read the Scriptures (audibly, if possible). Read them the way you would picture a lover reading a love-letter from his beloved. Remember that every day you have the honor of sitting down with a book that contains the words of the One who created you, and who loved you enough to pay an infinite price to have a relationship with you. Go into the Holy of Holies each day, spread your Bible there on the Mercy Seat, and read it in the light of the bright Shekinah of God's Presence.

After you have read from the Scriptures, pray the passage in paraphrase back to God. My mother used to say, "It is impolite to change the subject when someone is talking to you." How much more impolite if we change the subject on God! (Check the prayers at the end of a typical church service by this standard. God has just spoken through a message from His Word, and we often pray our own rote prayers which focus a million miles from His address. Surely, this is serious sin against the Romance God wants with us!). Pray God's truth back to Him until His will becomes your will at all points of His address to you. Listen as a lover to his beloved, and talk as a child to his father. It is wise to take notes on any message you hear from God or about God, and then pray back over it. Then, read the selection for that day from the daily devotional book, letting God speak through it. Then, engage in specific prayer, possibly following the acrostic, **ACTS**: **A** for adoration, a response to the *greatness* of God; **C** for confession, a response to the *holiness* of God: **T** for thanksgiving, a response to the *goodness* of God; and **S** for supplication, a response to the *generosity* of God. As you conclude this time with God, ask Him to allow you to carry the awareness of His Presence and His revealed will with you all through the day.

William Blake, the puzzling poet, wrote,

"I give you the end of a golden string,
Only wind it into a ball,
It will lead you in at Heaven's gate,
Inside Jerusalem's wall."

If Blake's poem is intended to be about salvation, then it is both false and misleading. But if it can be used as a quiet time formula, it will serve to remind us that the discipline of the quiet time is as nothing compared to the delight of its rewards.

VI. The PURPOSE of it

Sixth, what is the *purpose* of the quiet time with God? In the burning bush story of Exodus 3, it was only after Moses "turned aside" to see this unusual sight that God revealed Himself to him. The quiet time is for the purpose of "turning aside" to meet with God. The primary purpose of the quiet time is not for gathering principles or gleaning spiritual produce, but *to cultivate relationship with a Person*, to have a heart occupied with Christ. It is to cultivate *a spiritual romance with Him*, in the truest sense of the word romance. Elizabeth O'Connor said, "We are called first of all to belong to Jesus

Christ as Savior and Lord, and to keep our lives warmed at the hearth of His life." "The Bible is not as much exposure to precepts as it is an encounter with a Person." The greatest incentive to the practice of the daily quiet time is not to get your needs met; it is to look away from all else and unto Jesus (Heb. 12:2, and especially II Cor. 3:18). Spend your life mastering II Cor. 3:18, which is, to me, the greatest motto verse in the Bible in understanding the Christian life and its practical implementation.

An anointed preacher was asked by an admirer, "Where did you attend school?" The preacher answered, "I went to Mary's College." "Mary's College?" the enquirer asked. "Where is Mary's College?" "It is in the thirty-ninth verse of Luke chapter ten," the preacher replied, "which says that 'Mary sat at the feet of Jesus, and heard His word." The best theology degree in the world is gained in "Mary's College"!

There was a day in Napoleon's life in which disaffection had arisen in his men, and mutiny was threatened. Napoleon sat alone in a little room with two doors. Into one door came his men, one by one, and Napoleon clasped the hand of each and looked him full in the face for a passionate moment. The problem was over. Our Commander, Jesus, is summoning us to Himself, one by one. He wants to look us full in the face and let us feel the gentle love-pressure of His nail-pierced hand. We should envision this reality in each daily quiet time. Let each encounter with God be a time of transparent dialogue, remembering that "The Lord is with you, while you are with Him" (II Chronicles 15:2, RSV).

VII. The PROTECTION of it

Finally, we must give great care to the *protection* of the daily quiet time. Remember the principle: *what counts costs!*

You will find that the most vicious attacks of the adversary will be directed toward robbing you of your daily time with God. *You* may not appreciate this time fully, but *Satan* does! You will have to guard it fearlessly if you are to keep it. It will need to be guarded from: your own delinquencies, distractions, drowsiness, dispositional deficiencies, and other enemies. Samuel Logan Brengle, the successor to William Booth as the Commanding General of the Salvation Army, said, "I have only one temptation in ministry—it's the temptation to want to do something for God each day, before I've first spent time with Him." This temptation must be resisted as the most deadly of all temptations.

In the economy of God, "go *hide* thyself" (I Kings 17:3) comes *before* "go *show* thyself" (I Kings 18:1). Effective *public* ministry will only follow efficient *private* ministry. L. Nelson Bell said, "Don't keep forever on the public road. Leave the beaten path for a short time each day and drive into the woods. Then you will be refreshed for the rest of the journey, even if you are facing a hard drive to your destination." If we hide ourselves daily in the Presence of God, as Elijah did in obeying God, we will fare well in the encounters with the Ahabs of life. If not, we must "sponsor ourselves"—and take the losses!

Dr. Raymond Edman was speaking to Wheaton College chapel about how we should prepare to meet with God, when suddenly he slumped onto the pulpit, fell to the floor....and entered into the Presence of the King! How would we approach tomorrow morning's quiet time if we knew we would actually die while in it—and *actually enter face-to-face into the King's Presence*? One day we will meet together in the King's Presence. Let's make sure that we are not on unfamiliar territory or in strange company when that day comes!

SUPPORTIVE QUOTES AND ILLUSTRATIONS ON THE QUIET TIME

Francis Carr Stifler went to Chicago to call on a Lutheran pastor, whose work, according to a news magazine article, was attended by unusual success. The accuracy of the report was borne out. Although the church members had recently built a new building — one they had felt would be adequate for many years — they now were having to conduct three morning services to take care of the crowds. There was a constant stream of people uniting with the church by baptism. The church was having no problems with finances. All of this in the face of the fact that this was an old downtown church. When asked for the secret of such a phenomenon, the pastor attributed the success mainly to one thing. "I have persuaded ninety percent of my families to have regular family prayers." The church had twenty-nine hundred families in its local membership. This meant that about twenty-six hundred families in the membership of the church were having family worship. When asked how he persuaded such a large percentage of his people to do this, the pastor said that he had personally taught most of his families to do it; he had gone from house to house, as many times as required, until they were willing to continue with the experience. (J. Winston Pearce)

One of the best ways to teach someone how to have a quiet time is to do it together. This is the "with Him" principle of Mark 3:14: "Jesus appointed twelve, that they might be with Him." Early in your relationship meet together with your disciple in special sessions to have a quiet time together. Pick a time that is suitable to you both. Don't pressure him into having it the same time you do. Remember, the time isn't sacred. Then lead him through a quiet time. Show the disciple how to pray and how to read God's Word. Every disciple should be encouraged to read the Bible systematically, and every disciple should be encouraged to keep a prayer list as an aid in making his prayer time more balanced and specific. (Roy Peterson)

A hurried quiet time will yield predictable results. In a Peanuts cartoon, Lucy told Charlie Brown, "I just completed a course in speed reading and last night I read <u>War and Peace</u> in one hour! . . . It was about Russia." (Kent Hughes)

A certain man could not find the right posture for prayer. He tried praying on his knees, but that was not comfortable; besides, it wrinkled his slacks. He tried praying standing, but soon his legs got tired. He tried praying seated, but that did not seem reverent. Then one day as he was walking through a field, he fell headfirst into an open well. And did he ever pray! (Kent Hughes)

Robert Munger preaches a message called "My Heart, Christ's Home." It tells of the various rooms in the heart of one who has come to know the Lord. One of those rooms is most important. It is a small room, at the bottom of the stairs, just off to the side. That is the room where the Lord says to the new believer, "Here I will meet with you each morning." Many of us have learned the blessing of making our way to that room, morning after morning, to be with the Lord. To pray. To study His Word in Scripture. Simply to sit and enjoy being in His presence. But most of us also know that on some mornings we oversleep. We let the pressure of other things detour us from our regular time with the Lord. Day after day we rush down the stairs and out the front door, forgetting about the small room off to the side. Until one day we notice the door to that room slightly ajar and the light on inside. We peer inside — and there is the Lord, sitting there all alone.

"Lord," we say, "what are *you* doing here?" "Waiting for you," he replies. "Have you forgotten?" (D. James Kennedy)

I hated doing it, but I kept on getting up at 6:30 A.M. for my hour with the Lord. I got nothing out of it and I told Him so. But I got up anyway and now I know that every syllable of the Word of God which we drop into our subconscious minds stays there and becomes a *usable part* of us! Even if we don't seem to get it with our conscious minds. (Eugenia Price)

Our perpetual temptation in any Christian work is to let the work take priority over our personal walk with Christ. We are always conscious of the pressures to put the work first. That is so easy to justify. The reality, though, is that we always move from serving in His resources, gained from intimacy with Him, to ministry that arises from our own strength alone. Our security against such a drift is the development of personal devotional habits that keep Him central and that maintain a perpetual inflow of His life and character. We must know the resurrected Christ and commune with Him each day. (Dennis Kinlaw)

We are inundated in words. They form the floor, walls, and ceiling of our lives. Words scream at us from radios, TVs, billboards, bumper stickers, and announcements. One author said that while driving through Los Angeles he had the strange sensation of driving through a dictionary: "use me, take me, buy me, drink me, eat me, smell me, touch me, kiss me, sleep with me." Words gone wild. Words tangle us up with this world and put out the inner fire within us. Our spiritual life is like a steam bath. When we open the door, the room loses its heat. When we are always talking, the fire of the spirit within us cools. Make silence a violent obsession. (Henri Nouwen)

Occasionally I am asked what I would like to pass on to the next generation of Christians. My reply: maintain at all costs a daily time of Scripture reading and prayer. As I look back, I see that the most formative influence in my life and thought has been my daily contact with Scripture over sixty years. (Frank Gaebelein)

The key to the Christian's engagement with the world or in Christian work is the Christian's engagement with God. (Bill Hull)

"Allan, I should have told you this a long time ago. Do you remember the first time we stopped at this hotel in 1953? Rooms were scarce and we shared a twin-bedded room. That night, before retiring, you popped out a Bible and began reading. I asked if you would read out loud. That was just ten years ago. As we traveled about I asked that you read to me morning and evening. Since that time I have never missed a day in the Scriptures nor in having a time of prayer. Previously I was a churchman but I did not take faith very seriously. These past ten years have been totally different. My reading has changed. My priorities have changed. My life has been changed. I just wanted you to know." (Letter received by Allan Emery)

During the years it has been my practice to read from the Bible daily. It has been more than reading. Quite literally, it has been to "read, mark, learn, and inwardly digest" the subject matter. Among the many legacies left me by the small, evangelical college which I attended was the insistence on a life of devotion. There, long ago, the habit of devotion — approximately two hours a day of Bible study and prayer — was fixed. To this, maturity and refinement — the habit of listening to the Inner Voice as well as speaking during prayer — have been added. If I have had a secret weapon, this has been it. The margins of one Bible after another have literally

The Daily Quiet Time

been covered by the notes I have been accustomed to making along the way in my quiet time. These, as well as notes from my rather wide reading and recollection of the day's experiences taken down each night, have contributed to my sermons and books. There the seed was sown. (E. Stanley Jones)

It is imperative that the growing Christian develop a consistent devotional life. A daily time alone with God is a basic step in developing a close walk with God. It is in this time of intimate communion with God that we learn the most about Him, His will for our lives, His guidance, and His nature. Men of God agree that this daily time of devotions is the most important part of their day. The Word of God mentions in many places the need for a time alone with God and His Word. "I rise before dawn and cry for help; I hope in thy words. My eyes are awake before the watches of the night, that I may meditate upon thy promise" (Ps. 119:147,148). "His delight is in the law of the Lord, and on his law he meditates day and night" (Ps. 1:2). "Like newborn babes, long for the pure milk of the Word that by it you may grow" (I Peter 2:2). Prayer, the second area for disciplined obedience, is verbal communication with God — just talking with Him. God has established the exercise of prayer to enable us to respond to Him and communicate with Him. It is the second part of the divine communication process. The first part is God speaking to us through His Word and His Spirit. The second part is our responding back to Him in prayer. I have found that prayer is often misunderstood by the new Christian. He usually thinks of it as something that is dependent upon the right liturgy, terminology, or ritual. It is important to show him that prayer is simply a matter of talking with God. We don't need to know any complicated terminology or ritual. God desires for us to simply talk to Him. (Gary Kuhne)

In an interview with C.S. Lewis, Sherwood Wirt asked, "What is your view of the daily discipline of the Christian life — the need for taking time to be alone with God?" Lewis replied, "We have our New Testament regimental orders upon the subject. I would take it for granted that everyone who becomes a Christian would undertake this practice. It is enjoined upon us by our Lord; and since they are His commands, I believe in following them. It is always just possible that Jesus Christ meant what He said when He told us to seek the secret place and to close the door." (Selected Essays)

The moment you wake up each morning, all your wishes and hopes for the day rush at you like wild animals. And the first job each morning consists in shoving it all back; in listening to that other voice, taking that other point of view, letting that other, larger, stronger, quieter life come flowing in. (C. S. Lewis)

Many believers treat this discipline as if they misread "a quiet time every day" for "quinine every day." (Kent Hughes)

When I talk to certain people about their quiet time with God, I sometimes get the feeling that their brains work like taxi meters that translate time and effort into money — and that they think of investing time in God's Word as less profitable than work-related activity. They talk of squeezing in a few minutes to read their Bibles before hitting the road or praying as they sit in traffic. Their spiritual nourishment reminds me of an "instant breakfast" — quick, easy, with all the basic nutrients and vitamins, but not very exciting or creative... and not really sufficient for the long haul. (Dave Gilbert)

These profitable insights are recorded in Hugh Evan Hopkins' excellent little book entitled <u>Henceforth</u>: "The practical side to victory over sin lies in the keeping of a Quiet Time with God. It is then that faith is fed and holiness cultivated and victories won. Nothing in the life of the Christian is more attacked than his times alone with his God. Yet nothing is more essential if he is to go forward in the spiritual life. Frequent interviews with his Master are the secret of abiding in him. All the saints of the past have been men who have made time to see their King's face. John Wesley and Charles Simeon were up by four in the morning; Bishop Ken and Samuel Rutherford are reputed to have risen earlier still; Lancelot Andrews spent five hours a day in his devotions; Gordon of Khartoum used to tie a while handkerchief outside his tent door during his Quiet Time and no one was allowed to disturb him.

"The essential point is determination and sincerity of purpose rather than length of time. The closed door and the quiet spirit are what the Father requires of his children when they would meet with him." (Page 46)

When I took up jogging for a time (before ankle injuries drove me to walking and biking), runner-friends kept telling me, "Jogging is great! It makes you feel better!" Well, it didn't always make me feel better. Sometimes it made me sore and cranky. What kept me committed was the understanding that jogging wasn't so much for my immediate benefit as for my long-term health. Devotion to God requires a similar commitment. Seeking Him daily doesn't depend on our feelings. "The word of God is living and active and sharper than any two-edged sword, and piercing as far as the division of soul and spirit, of both joints and marrow, and able to judge the thoughts and intentions of the heart." This kind of surgery may not always feel wonderful, but it does wonders for our spiritual health. (Philip Wiebe)

Learning to focus your attention on Jesus throughout the day often proves to be hard work. It will not happen quickly and immediately. The following steps will help you to begin experiencing fellowship with the Lord more often during your day.

Anticipate. Expect to experience fellowship with Christ throughout the day.

Thank. "In everything give thanks."

Talk. Talk to God about everything — problems, questions, choices and responsibilities.

Enjoy. Make it your constant purpose just to enjoy Jesus.

Notice. Look for God at work in your life and in the people and events around you.

Think. Think about God and His Word at all possible times.

Imagine. "Image" your walk with God in your mind, imagining Him to be right beside you.

Open. Open your mouth as often as possible to speak and sing about the Lord.

Need. Admit your need of God, and be satisfied with nothing short of fellowship with Him.

(Author undocumented)

The greatest thing anyone can do for God and for man is to pray. It is not the only thing. But it is the chief thing. The great people of the earth today are the people who pray. I do not mean those who talk about prayer; nor those who say they believe in prayer; nor yet those who can explain about prayer; but I mean those people who take time and pray. They have not time. It must be taken from something else. This something else is important. Very important and pressing, but still less important and less pressing that prayer. (S. D. Gordon)

Prayer will make a man cease from sin, or sin will entice a man to cease from prayer. You may test your life by which one prevails, sin or prayer. (John Bunyan)

You can do more than pray *after* you have prayed, but you cannot do more than pray *until* you have prayed. (John Bunyan)

God never denied that soul anything that went as far as heaven to ask for it. (John Trapp)

God always uses the vessel that lies closest at hand. (Author undocumented)

Chapter 2

THE MATTER OF AN INTIMATE RELATIONSHIP WITH GOD

Sometime ago, I received in a letter a series of questions which triggered much thought in my mind and gave me incentive to explore and explain. The questions all had to do with "an intimate relationship with God." I have received such questions in some form or another several times, but seldom (if ever) in such a close succession. I want to address some of them in this vignette.

"Does the Bible teach that we can have an intimate relationship with God?" My answer was, of course, *Yes*. It not only teaches that we *can* have an intimate relationship with God, it teaches that the only possible *real* relationship with God is the intimate relationship. This is why the New Birth is a "must" (John 3:3, 7), because without it, man has no relationship with God at all. Though the unsaved man lives out his entire life with God as his "frame of reference," he has no relationship with God until he is born again. By means of the New Birth, man receives the very life of God within himself and *is thus brought into identification* (a more intimate relationship with *anything* or *anyone* is not possible) and *union* with God.

In John 17:3, Jesus said to His Father, "This is life eternal, that men may know You the only true God, and Jesus Christ Whom You have sent." The word "know" is exactly the same word that is used in the Septuagint (Greek) Version of the Old Testament in such verses as Genesis 4:1, "Adam *knew* Eve his wife, and she conceived and gave birth to Cain." The word "knew" pictures in both cases the greatest possible intimacy, a physical intimacy in the case of Adam and Eve and a spiritual intimacy in the case of man with God. But the word in each case is an expression of the deepest possible intimacy. Yes, it is fully possible and absolutely necessary for one human being to have an intimate relationship with God. The old catechism question and answer said it well, "The chief end of man is to know God and to enjoy Him forever." It might also be added that one of the chief purposes of *God* is *to know man and to enjoy him forever!*

"Where in the Bible can we find examples of human beings experiencing an intimate relationship with God?" My answer was, *On page after page.* I want to preface my explanation at this point with a few necessary remarks. Most people seem to have a terrible misunderstanding of "an intimate relationship with God." They seem to think that such a relationship must always be perfect or there is no relationship at all. In my measured understanding, this *mis*understanding is the product of very shallow thought. When human beings are involved in a (any) relationship, they always prevent its perfection because they are sinners, and the distortion of being sinners necessarily twists to some degree any relationships they may have. This is the reason man needs to be saved, and the reason salvation *is/must be* by *Grace.* Without grace, without God acting toward man in grace and mercy,

The Matter of an Intimate Relationship with God

there could be no salvation at all. This is what makes the message of Christianity a "Gospel". It is the Best News any man can ever hear, know and experience. The Gospel tells us that, despite man's helplessness and hopelessness in sin, God has graciously acted to open the way for man to come into intimacy with Himself. Later in this series of vignettes, it is my hope to show why the awareness of this Gospel may be the most important factor in establishing a climate, an atmosphere for daily intimacy with God.

My relationship with my wife is certainly not perfect (after all, my wife is a *woman*—a quite admirable Divine arrangement, but one that throws into the relationship an often baffling "mix"—and she would firmly admit the same thing with regard to me, a *man*), but in spite of its imperfection, my relationship with my wife is intimate. We both are aware of the absence of perfection in our relationship (we have not yet found a way to surmount that difficulty), though we work constantly to improve our relationship. The mutual effort we put into the maintenance of our relationship creates a deeper understanding of each other, and creates in each of us a greater appreciation for each other. Any relationship requires careful and regular attention, and the same is true of one's relationship with God. I work steadily to adjust my relationship with God, correcting any breakdown or distortion I am aware of, and maintaining the disciplines of the relationship as regularly as I can. The human imperfections in any relationship, properly understood and accepted (without excuse or extenuation), *still do not detract from intimacy in that relationship.* The Gospel of the grace of God assures me that every deficiency is covered—if I am intent on "leaning toward Him" as I take the successive steps of my daily pilgrimage.

Biblically, the spotlight of our attention might be thrown upon the stories of Enoch in Genesis 5:21-24, a story of remarkable intimacy with God. And that of Abraham in Genesis 15 through 21, as well as the story of Moses in the book of Exodus. Note in every case that the relationships of these believers with God were not perfect, but were always covered by the grace of God. Throughout the Bible, one person after another had a believing, struggling, singing, shouting, *protesting*, etc., relationship with God—and the protesting was often the greatest show of intimacy, because it showed how much God meant to the believer. Carnal, timid people tend to *ignore* God because of their own failures, but truly spiritual people engage in full, honest and real relationships with Him, and *especially so when they are aware of failure*. Some of the signs and symptoms of these relationships are positive, some are negative, but they are *intimate*. I have been engaging in a Quiet Time examination of the book of Job for nearly a year now. The thing that has most impressed me about Job is his open, honest, uninhibited exchange with God in the most intimate possible way, while always maintaining personal confidence that God has final dispatch of all matters and is open to our approach with any matter we want to bring to him. Job's intimacy with God is the feature that allowed a major subtle change to occur in him (Job) in the last chapters of the incredible book that bears Job's name. The same will happen with any human being who engages in regular intimacy with God. He will discover vistas of mystery and mercy, love and grace, disclosure and honesty, that he never would have known apart from such a relationship.

I do not mean to leave the impression that intimacy with God was most evident only in Old Testament characters. The lives of all of the Apostles of Christ were marked by intimate exchanges with Him—in conversation, in observa-

The Matter of an Intimate Relationship with God

tion, in learning, in communion, etc. It was through the deepest scrutiny of personal intimacy that they arrived at their Spirit-taught conclusions about His identity, His integrity, His Purpose, etc. It was this intimacy that established the "power base" of their lives and enabled them later to "turn the world upside down." One has only to read the extensive accounts of John, Peter, Paul and others to see great examples of intimacy with God through Jesus Christ.

"How would you define an intimate relationship with God?" It is surely something of an oversimplification, but I would begin with the word Jesus used. Intimate relationship with God or with Jesus Christ can be defined as "abiding." It would be valuable here to read and/or re-read John 15:1-8 and I John 2:28 as examples of the use of this word. Someone interpreted this as "centering" on Jesus Christ all day long every day. This is a good definition, even if it requires much amplification. This brings into the picture all the "means of grace", all the supportive means of relationship-building and relationship maintenance, that are essential. The list includes the daily dependent study of the Word of God, turning the Bible into a territory of encounter and intimacy, not a mere object of academic study. Another means of relationship is open, realistic prayer, the "talking" and communing side of the relationship. Another is fellowship and worship with other believers who are engaged in an open, all-cylinders-active, relationship with God. Another is witnessing and soul-winning, an activity in which God "jumps rails" and joins you so that the intimacy of relationship is enhanced. The one setting I have often found to be very quickening of my own relationship with Him is the open, free, uninhibited small group of disciples in a disciple-making setting, expressing transparency, freedom, happiness and honesty together as expressions of their own free relationship with Jesus. I have left many meetings of such disciples wonderfully aware of the near Presence of our Lord, more intimately aware of His Person and His Purpose, and more determined to know and serve Him better. "While we were musing, the fire burned."

Perhaps this vignette will "open the door" for the coming "Suggestions About "How to Improve Your Daily Quiet Time."

Chapter 3

LESSONS TO CARRY TO THE PRAYER CLOSET

Let me begin this vignette with a clear lesson that has glared at me from my Quiet Time sessions in the book of Job recently, then follow the opening lesson with a series of lessons that were suggested by the first one.

First, when going to your "prayer closet" (Matthew 6:6), *remember who you **aren't**!* Somewhere I saw this quote, "There is only one God per universe, and in *this* universe, *I am not He!*" The very nature of sin is to put myself in God's place and try to occupy His throne and play His role. "You shall be like God," was Satan's first temptation, and he still utilizes it to his own advantage today. What a relief it is to settle the issue of Who is God! None of us is as important as all of us tend to think we are. Someone wisely said, "If you think of yourself 'more highly than you ought to think,' perform this simple exercise. Get a large bowl, fill it with water, thrust your finger into the water, remove it, and see how big a hole is left in the water." When this issue is settled for me in favor of truth, incalculable burdens are lifted from my shoulders. I no longer have to assume sole responsibility to govern myself, fret alone over my responsibilities and my schedule, and protest over barriers which seem insurmountable and burdens which seem unbearable. He is God, and He is *omnicompetent!* I am delivered from the stupidity and sin of replacing Him with my own pygmy effort.

Second, when going to your "prayer closet," *remember who you **are**!* Reinforce the first lesson by remembering that you are a limited, dependent man, and that the Lord Almighty is the sole and only God. Then take a giant step in the admission of who you are *before God, in Christ*. If you are a twice-born child of God, gigantic derivative realities define and describe you.

One is that you are a child of God both by birth (which has given you a new nature) and by adoption (which has given you a new standing and new privileges).

Another is that you are indwelt by a "Stay-within Friend," the Holy Spirit of God. Remember that your body is the "Holy of Holies" (the exact meaning of the word translated "temple" in I Corinthians 6:19) in which God literally dwells. Remember that you are a perpetual carrier of the Presence of God in the mediating Presence of the Holy Spirit. You may feature yourself going into your prayer closet to *meet* God, but the truth is that you are *carrying Him into the prayer closet* and you are going there to be reminded of the possibility of intimate relationship with Him *all of the time*. Without the regular encounters with Him there, you tend to forget that He is in you and with you wherever you go.

A third reality that derives from your new birth is that you have been sealed in Christ by the Holy Spirit, and thus may have full assurance that you are secure in Christ and will be delivered fully safe to Heaven when your journey on earth is complete. Also, simultaneous with that sealing, you were also given the "down-payment of the Spirit" to show you what is coming in "future installments" and to guarantee that you *will receive* all future increments of the inheritance that became yours when you were saved.

These truths provide only a beginning of "taking our inventory" as Christians.

Third, when going to your prayer closet, *remember what you **have**—both negatively and positively.* On the liability side of the ledger, the negative side, you still have *the flesh, with its horrible capability of acting like itself.* The flesh or "self-curl" that remains in you after you are saved is like a Jack-in-the-box just waiting to be released in your experience. The flesh has been described as "the beast in the basement," waiting for someone to open the cellar door and invite the beast to rise up and show off in the rest of the house—and in the neighborhood nearby. The "works of the flesh" are devastating in the believer's life, but they are always possible.

The presence of the flesh, which is "Satan's handle" in your life, allows the continuing capacity to commit flagrant sin at any time. When you hold that handle out toward Satan, he will be happy to take hold of it and drag you around at his will. Many a Christian has sadly lamented after some horrible sin, "I can't believe I did that," but his lament only reveals that he has not understood the flesh or has not been wise enough to keep the cellar door closed on God's terms.

On the "assets" side of the ledger, the positive understanding of what you have in Christ, the inventory list is great and glorious. I will mention just one item: you have the imminent companionship of Jesus. "I will never leave you nor forsake you," Jesus said in Hebrews 13:5. Grammatically, this sentence in Greek has *five negatives* in it! What pains Jesus has taken for us to assure and reassure us of His unbroken Presence with us!

An atheistic college student posted on his door a sign which arrogantly said, "God is nowhere!" But some simple Christian rearranged the letters in the announcement so that it read, "God is *now here!*" God is at the prayer closet door, ready to host your coming as you enter to meet with Him. Magnify His Presence, and then enjoy it as you linger with Him throughout your Quiet Time.

Furthermore, the Holy Spirit has told you in His Book that "all things are yours" (I Corinthians 3:21, 22). In that text, Paul then proceeds to give an itemized list of your possessions in Christ. The list is by no means *exhaustive*. In fact, it is certainly not the list of possessions any Christian would have devised, and this shows us how different God's evaluation is from ours. The eight items in the I Corinthians 3:21, 22 list are the most important things in the range of human experience, but no sinner will easily admit this. A Christian's wealth only shows up *as wealth* in the light of eternity – or in the light of Heaven's wisdom prevailing in a Christian's heart. Every Christian is absolutely and boundlessly rich with unfading and imperishable wealth, but he must "read his inventory" on a regular basis to be reminded of his riches.

Finally, when going to your "prayer closet," *remember where you are*. Let me quickly remind you of your spiritual location, wherever you may be geographically.

First, you are *in Christ*. Your residence is in Christ, your primary relationships are in Christ, your resources are in Christ, etc., etc. You are *sphered* in Christ, *surrounded* by Christ, *secured* in Christ, *safe* in Christ, *supplied* in Christ, etc., etc.

Second, you are *in the Body of Christ*. You are a "member in particular" of His very Body, the Church. You are so attached to Christ that you cannot be dismembered from Him. Furthermore, you are enlisted in the design He has for

His Body. Just as you, an invisible personality living in a visible body, perform and reveal yourself through your body, so does Jesus perform and reveal Himself through His Body. And *you are a crucial part of His performance and His self-revelation.* Celebrate this when you approach the door of your prayer closet, and praise Him for such an arrangement!

Third, and far more soberly, you are *still in the wicked world that crucified Christ.* Remember that this world "is no friend of grace," and that this world is both one of your leading obstacles in being a Christian, but also one of your leading opportunities for sharing Him with desperately lost people. The world is both your leading challenge in practicing your faith in Christ, your leading opportunity to make Him known, and your best workshop to magnify Him.

Finally, you are in a circle of brothers, sisters and friends, with whom you are to share mutual support as a Christian. Pray for those you remember as you bow at God's throne, and ask Him to make you a great support to each of them, and to allow each of them to be a great support to you.

Let me conclude by paraphrasing a paragraph from a book I am presently reading:

Psalm 62:8 says, "Pour out your hearts to Him, for God is our refuge." Human hearts tend to be full of many things, things such as joy, anger, peace, weariness, anxiety, strength, bitterness, trust,... To pour out the heart means to pour out not just some of these elements before the Lord, but all of them, the 'bad' as well as the 'good.' When we pray, everything in our hearts must be poured out to the Lord like a drink offering, so that the heart is kept empty for Him. You see, God comes Himself and brings His blessings to fill us, but He often finds our hearts already filled with many, many things and He cannot fulfill His purpose. "Pour out your heart to Him" so it will be empty to receive Him and all He brings.

Chapter 4

MASTER MOTTOES FOR APPROACHING GOD

In my Quiet Time one morning this week, I was introduced by Exchange With the Holy Spirit to several "master mottoes" for approaching God. Let me share them with you in this vignette.

Motto Number One: "Lord, I am *all ears*." "I am *here* to *hear* from You."

On one occasion after another, Jesus addressed the master theme of "hearing." He said such things as, "He who has ears to hear, let him hear." He who *has ears* — that reveals the *capacity* of each person to hear. "He who has ears *to hear*" — that reveals the *possibility* of each person to hear. "He who has ears to hear, *let him hear*" — that reveals the *responsibility* of each person to hear. Then He said, "Let every man *be careful that he hear*" — that is, each person must give maximum regular attention to the crucial matter of hearing from God. And, "Let every man take heed *what he hears*" — that is, the Christian must listen discriminately, deliberately filtering out undesirable messages that arrive from anti-Christian sources.

The Daily Quiet Time

And, "Let every man take heed *how he hears"*— that is, every believer is responsible to culture and develop his listening, in order to maximize the Word that God sends on a regular basis to challenge and change him. Jesus talked *a great deal* about hearing; it seems to have been very important to Him that we learn how to listen. This must not be taken for granted. Why is this so very important?

A Manhattan couple sat at the breakfast table reading parts of the daily newspaper. He suddenly exclaimed, "It says here that a man is run over in New York every half hour." Absorbed in her part of the paper, the wife half-heartedly answered, "Goodness! You'd think by this time he'd learn to look when he's crossing the road!" Dear Christian, learn this principle: Communication is not what the speaker is saying. Rather, it is what the listener is hearing. And this is true even when the Speaker is God!

You see, without a miracle, we hear only what we are prepared to hear, or only what is comfortable to hear. In fact, without a miracle, we won't hear from God on His frequency at all. "Faith comes by hearing, and hearing by the word (*rhema*, the heart-penetrating, spirit-quickening word) of God." Without that miracle of heart penetration and spirit quickening, we may read reams of print on the page of the Bible—and never hear from God.

American songwriter Frank Loesser was asked how he got the ideas for his songs. He answered, "My head is arranged to receive songs." Christian, how is your head arranged with regard to God? And more importantly, *your heart?*

A young Christian visited a veteran Spirit-walking Christian who was renowned in the Christian community for his wisdom. The young Christian boldly said, "I have heard of your wisdom as a Christian, and I want to ask what is the secret of it?" The wise Christian said, "Listen"—and that's all he said. True wisdom lies in listening to God. The Christian must learn to listen to God deliberately, a matter of the *head*. He must listen deeply, a matter of the *heart*. And he must listen dynamically, devotedly and directionally, a matter of the *habit*.

Two men were talking. One asked, "Does your wife ever talk to herself?" The other answered cleverly, "Yes, but she doesn't *know* it; *she thinks I'm listening.*" Loosen the definition a bit and we can easily see that God must do a lot of talking to Himself!

One day sometime ago, my wife gently said to me, "Honey, why is it that you can remember what you read in a book thirty-five years ago, and even whether it was on the right hand page or left hand page and which paragraph down the page— and you can't remember what I said to you five minutes ago?" I took advantage of her gentleness and answered unwisely, "Motivation, my dear, motivation! Or I guess you could call it 'selective intake.'" Honestly, we both laughed because of the spirit of the moment, but that exchange kept lingering in my mind. How many times have I practiced 'selective intake,' either wittingly or unwittingly, with God? May God have mercy upon me! I wonder how much I have missed His merciful revelation because of my botched listening?

The New Testament discloses vast frontiers that are obviously closed to most Christians because we listen only to the limit of our preconceptions and previous conditioning. And this is also true of Christian leaders (all of them), unless they keep themselves consciously and miraculously open to God's full disclosure. I know that in my own experience God has had to smash my early limited understanding (though it was set in stone) in order to disclose what He was really saying. The truth is that the quality of my listening may effectually reduce what He is saying, and the tenure of my listening has little to do with it. In fact, my presumption as a long-time listener may be deadly to my understanding of His full revelation. So called "conviction" may preclude further communication. We are responsible to listen, but do we? How well do we listen when the air is full of the waves of His speech, and His Manual, the Bible, is handy as the full specification and clarification of what He wants to say? Motto Number One reminds me that I, the potential hearer, must make plenty of room for the Speaker and Everything He Says. "Lord, I am all ears."

Motto Number Two: Lord, I am willing to be *ears* and *mouth*

I will just briefly mention Motto Number Two, though it deserves better treatment than that. Motto Number Two is: "Lord, I am willing to be ears *and mouth."* However, I want to attach a proviso because of my weakness in the flesh—"if only You would so determine my listening that my speech is essentially a repetition of what You are saying."

Sometime ago, I heard Dave Feherty, commentator on the Professional Golf Association's tournament telecasts, say something clever about Scottish golfer Colin Montgomery: "Sometimes Colin sends his brain on vacation and leaves his mouth in control at home." Ouch! How many times have I done this in conversation, in domestic situations, in casual speech, in "clever" speech, in teaching and preaching, and even in my Quiet Time!

Sometime ago, I was blessed beyond description by a quick reading of Eugene Peterson's paraphrase of the New Testament called, <u>The Message</u>. I couldn't put it down until I had read it through. I marked the "keeper passages" and went back and recorded them in my illustration file. I was "stopped in my tracks" by this paraphrase of a great passage in the book of James: "Post this at all the intersections: Lead with your ear, follow up with your tongue, and let anger struggle along in the rear." Dismiss the last sentence for the moment—it is usually better to unhitch the anger trailer altogether! "Lead with your ear, and follow up with your tongue." Why should not a Christian simply be a conduit for the Speech of God? But we must sadly admit that this is usually not true of us because we typically put our tongues in motion before our hearts are in gear! If I am to be a channel for the speech of God, I must take extreme care to "lead with my ear."

Motto Number Three: *"Lord, I am all ears"*

So the third Motto is the same as the first. It enables me to bracket my speech (my one mouth) with my listening to God (symbolized by my *two* ears). *"Lord, I am all ears,"* and I want to (as an illustration) use one ear on one side of my speaking and the other ear on the other, using one ear before my speech and one ear after my speech. In this way, I can be more certain that my speech is a reflection of what I am hearing from God.

Sadly, the typical "hearing pattern" of most Christians in church creates a "glut" of truth. It has been said, "The congregation in church is just as responsible to *master the sermon and leave with it* as the pastor is to *master it before he arrives with it.*" Weigh these words carefully, and confess that the typical Christian has not the slightest awareness of this "hearing vocation." Instead, multitudes of church members listen casually to God's attempt to communicate truth to them and seek only (at best) to extract a "blessing" or an "inspiration" or an "enjoyment" from it. They do not linger over the truth of what they have heard to translate it from *ears* to *heart* to *knees* to *feet*. Hardly realizing that they are actually compounding their guilt by irresponsible listening in church, they go their ways, perhaps to come back on Sunday evening and *enlarge the glut* (and the *guilt*). No wonder the Christian movement in the western world limps along at such a pitiful pace when it could be regularly riding a giant tide of spiritual power – and its limp begins in the Prayer Closet in the way it hears (perhaps more accurately, *doesn't hear*) from God! As usual, *the prayer closet will determine the public course.* No use of the prayer closet, no power in the public course. Little private prayer, little public power.

Christian, may we pledge ourselves together today to urgently ask God for sanitized (clean) and sensitized (committed) listening as we touch the handle of our Prayer Closets? A young boy approached the metal detector at the airport. He started around it. The guard was under the table at the moment, attaching a sign to the edge of the inspection table. From his knees, the guard called out abruptly, "No, son, you'll have to come through this way." The little boy dropped to his knees and crawled through under the table! Oh, if we could just be that teachable, that simple, that resilient, that trusting, that responsible before God!

The primary Greek word for obedience (*hupokoia; akoia* is the word from which we get our word "acoustics") is a compound word which means "to listen underneath." What a picture: obedience begins with submitted, humble listening, listening that is exercised *underneath* the total Lordship of Christ. Jesus set the mode when He said, "I do only and exactly what I hear my Father say." Perhaps this is the first step to take in our aspirations to be Christ-like. "I listen to my Father and live to do what He says." Let's approach the Prayer Closet in the morning with new motivation!

Chapter 5

READING PRAYER

When you read the subtitle at the top of the page, your tendency will be to *mis*read it. I am not talking about the practice of reading prayers that have been written out prior to the time of prayer. I often journal (write out) my prayers in my early morning Quiet Time, and I have often been greatly blessed as I have gone back much later and read the written prayers (this is the subject of another vignette), but that is not the meaning of the title. This brief observation has to do with *turning your reading into prayer*.

Every Christian should have spiritual reading habits that penetrate every day, if possible. Years ago, I heard a saintly old Christian say, "The best way to pray is to read the Word, let God speak to you from it, and repeat or paraphrase back to Him what He is saying—with surrender to Him and the truth He has given to us and with thanksgiving for Him/it." I was instructed (and intimidated) years ago by reading the biography of George Mueller of Bristol, England, the great "man of faith" who sponsored several large orphanages for years merely by depending on God for their support.

43

The Daily Quiet Time

The remarkable story included this line: "He read the Bible completely through over seventy-five time on his knees." I am not the person to question that, challenge that, or seek to imitate that, but I do want to learn and be inspired from it. Personally, I cannot read the Bible and be warmed by its fire without reciprocally communicating with its Author on the basis of the Truth just received. I'm sure Mr. Mueller would have abandoned the habit of daily-Bible-reading-on-his-knees if it had not stimulated personal exchange with God.

My mother used to say to me, "When someone speaks to you, it is impolite to change the subject, and the more important the speaker is, the more important the rule is—don't change the subject." This is simply great sense; I would say "*common* sense," but it just happens that common sense has become about the most *un*common thing there is! Dear Christian, ask this question and apply this test: How many times have powerfully anointed church services ended with prayers that are more *rote* than *relationship*, more *regular* than a reflection of Divine-human *romance*? As a pastor for many years, I made the mistake of entrusting the closing prayer to many a "Hallelujah" service over to a "humdrum" pray-er. "Reading prayer" means that you cultivate the habit of "talking back" to God on the basis of the live words He has just spoken to you, and talking back with the same passion with which He addressed you.

Of course, this habit should begin with your reading and study of the Bible. During these immediate days, I am reading/studying the twenty-fourth of Luke, the great story of the Emmaus Walk Jesus took with two common disciples. *What a story!!!* At every dramatic twist and turn, I have looked up from the page and let my thoughts be drowned in praise and worship. I have thanked God with every sentence that I am privileged to know this story and use is as a model for my own walk with Him. I have recited the principles, the patterns, etc., of the passage and asked God to powerfully 'inflesh' them *in me*. How many times have I thought (and said), "Wow, this is mine! Jesus, this is You and me! This is the model for every Christian. My feet touch the Emmaus Road with every step I take. Please, do not let my eyes be 'holden' as theirs were; instead, let them be 'opened' by the Miracle of the Spirit's Grace, as theirs were."

This is "reading prayer," that is, prayer that is formed (and forced) and fired and fueled by the reading of that moment.

I want to be very cautious as I proceed "the rest of the way" in this vignette. Reading prayer should not only characterize your reading of the Bible. It should also be used in/during *everything you read*. Certainly, it should apply to all the devotional books you use to fuel your Quiet Time and your relationship with God. How many times have I recited, repeated, paraphrased, and rewritten in other words (the margins of all of my books look like the "scribble terrain" of a writer who is a hundred miles from notebook paper), the content of a daily devotional from Oswald Sanders' *My Utmost For His Highest*. I have often prayed, "Lord, you have given '*Your* Utmost for *my* highest,' now, please transform me so I can give '*my* utmost for *Your* highest!" I have heard from God out of those pages again and again, and again and again I have transposed the words of the text into the words of my lips/heart as I repeat them back to God in awe, wonder, brokenness, praise and worship. I have had at least an equal experience in the use of Glyn Evans' *Daily With the King*. I have been absolutely stupefied at the consistent Divine speech that has resonated in my heart from the daily use of these two books. "When an Important Person speaks to you, don't change the subject!" Never has my mother's dictum

The Daily Quiet Time

meant more to me than today. *"Child of God, don't change the subject when God speaks!"* Exhaust all possibilities inwardly and in exchange with Him to maximize what He is saying. When you get to the vignette based on "Buy the truth and sell it not," remember this vignette. Treat the immediate truth God speaks to you like a woman-with-a-new-diamond treats that diamond, turning it over in the sunlight to examine every facet of it, then re-turning it as if she has missed one or as if she would invent one that isn't even there! "Search the (reading) daily," and repeat the surface truths, the subtleties, the innuendos, back to God with a heart-shout of praise.

Now, here's the rub of this brief meditation. I personally believe this can/should be done by a Christian *with all reading*, not merely his "devotional" or "spiritual" reading. Reading prayer can be triggered by the newspaper. How many times have I heard my wife respond with prayer to a *happy* or a *horrible* news report while holding the daily newspaper spread open in her hands! "Lord, bless that …," "Lord, thank you for…," "Lord, please help those people …." How many times have we stopped our reading, recited the content to the other, then laid the newspaper down momentarily to pray for the people involved in some story. When we saw/read the first reports of the earthquake/tsunami in the area of the Indian Ocean, both of us wept and prayed as we tried to identify with the trauma-emotions and the devastation of the people of the area.

Every newscast should be a stimulant to prayer every day, every *National Geographic Special* or the specials on *The History Channel* should be used to intercede for the ethnic groups, cultures and nations featured, and every page read (of *anything*) should be a loud bell within a Christian ringing out "the call to prayer."

Another rub. I have found that literature-at-large is a great foundation for reading prayer. In another vignette, I have listed an entire category of short stories from great "classic authors" that have smashed my heart with great lessons of spiritual truth and strategy. I have read and re-read some of them many, many times, and have recited them again and again with one person, in small groups, in teaching settings, etc., etc. I have used their content as illustrations of the great truths of the Gospel over and over. But their appropriation, appreciation and application began with me, not just as a reading, but as reading *prayer*. Why should I "waste" such great truths as God has stimulated through the minds and pens of great writers just by an inward "thinking with the author" as I read? Why should I not also exchange with The Great Author of all truth as I read? And sometimes, I have prayed *negatively* over the reading, protesting the Spirit's disagreement with an untruth, a verbal or lingual abuse, etc. That is, *everything read causes a spiritual revolution within me.* I just want to be so insulated in Christ that anything disagreeable to His Presence will spread instantly throughout my character, and anything He approves can permeate me through and through. However, I do not want that insulation to become isolation. I want to be "in the world, but not of it," as Jesus said. I want to be *in* the world as a catalyst for His Cause, as a representative of His revelation, as a stimulus for spiritual life. All of this can be initiated by *reading prayer*; that is, by reading that is instantly turned into prayer.

Chapter 6

SUGGESTIONS FOR IMPROVING YOUR DAILY QUIET TIME

Number One: Remember the Gospel, and Let it Work on You First

Every married person knows that unbroken routine may be the enemy of relationship. "A rut is a grave with the ends knocked out." A highway sign in a western state said, "Choose your rut carefully, because you will be in it for the next twenty-five miles." A little creative thought will keep your Quiet Time from becoming stale and stagnant, from "rutting." In the next few vignettes, I want to address this matter.

Suggestion number one for improving your daily Quiet Time: *Go back to the basics on a regular basis*. The *Gospel* basics, not merely the devotional basics. Remind yourself to never tire of rehearsing the infinite dimensions of the glorious Gospel of Christ. "*I am a child of God because of the glorious*

The Daily Quiet Time

achievement of Jesus in my behalf." Then, spend a little time in each Quiet Time reviewing and celebrating that achievement in it many facets.

Daily read the Word, and wherever you are reading, turn to a tiny "Gospel passage" (such as Titus 2:11-14, Colossians 2:14-16, Hebrews 2:14-16, I Corinthians 15:1-10, Ephesians 2:1-10, as examples; keep an "address list" of the many great passages, and use at least one of them on a regular basis), and ask God to help you fully appreciate this "so great salvation" (Hebrews 2:3). To appreciate it so much that your heart wants to shout! What is the rationale behind this strategy? Why rehearse the Gospel on a daily basis? For this reason: if a believer *forgets* or *drifts away from* or *sins away the awareness of* the fact that "the blood of Jesus goes on cleansing up from all sin" (I John 1:7), his Quiet Time will become a shambles. If a believer forgets that Jesus has made full settlement of all of his sin-debt and all accounts that attend it, his Quiet Time is quickly subject to collapse. If a believer forgets that the Gospel provides coverage for the "now" of his daily life as well as for the "then" of his conversion, his Quiet Time likely will suffer. If a believer misses the ongoing blessings of the glorious Gospel of Christ for his daily victory (the fullness of the Spirit, victory over sin and the flesh, etc.), he may look up one day to sadly see that his Quiet Time is the leading casualty of the deadly deficiency. A defunct Quiet Time will lead to a defunct Christian walk, and the defunct walk will further lock the door of his prayer closet—it becomes a really vicious cycle manipulated by the Enemy. So the happy rehearsal of the glorious Gospel of Christ serves multiple preventive (and curative) purposes.

In my own Quiet Time one morning this week, I was reading devotionally from an author who mentioned Martin Luther, the great German reformer. He mentioned in a brief chapter "the radical, tenacious hold Luther had on the simple truth of the Gospel." Luther's renowned confession, "Here I stand, I can do no other," is a reflection of his two-fisted iron grip on the Gospel. Dear Christian, learn to think, walk, talk, eat, breathe, sleep, the Gospel all day long every day. It is an infinite and limitless and *glorious* subject; there is plenty of "thought material" to explore. The rehearsal of the Gospel on a regular basis tunes your heart to celebration and worship, and your Quiet Time offers the best platform to experience and express this. Your Quiet Time will enable you to "adorn the Gospel," but only if it is effective and powerful. Launching from a regular Gospel power-base will secure this.

Remember Who/what saved you. Remember Who/what first washed your sins away and ushered you perfectly clean into the Presence of God. Remember your first baby-fresh experience of Jesus and the Gospel. Remember the Word of Truth that first thundered in your soul in the grace and power of God. Remember that this simple/infinite message was what broke the chains of your captivity when you came to know the Liberator. Remember that this message is not one whit less powerful at this moment than it was at *that moment*. Keep going back to the basic message, the foundational Gospel. "Let us hold unswervingly to the hope we profess" (Hebrews 10:23). "Hold firmly to the trustworthy message as it has been taught" (Titus 1:9)."Just as you received Christ Jesus as Lord, continue to live in Him" (Colossians 2:6). The best way to grow in Christ and stay fresh in your relationship with Him is to keep going back to the first step you took in becoming a Christian and then repeat that step over and over again every day. Repentance and faith should be "perennial plants" in the Christian's Garden of Life. Trusting Jesus should mark every day's activities, moment by moment. The righteousness we have in Christ is "by faith from first to last" (Romans 1:17).

> "At the Cross, at the Cross, Where I first saw the light,
> And the burden of my heart rolled away;
> It was there by faith that I first saw the light,
> And NOW I am happy all the day."

All the writers of the New Testament launched their writings from this "pad of truth"—that justification by faith in Jesus Christ and His Finished Work is the only Gospel there is, and it is all we need now and forever.

Let this sentence stand as a description of the contrast we often see among Christians: "Perhaps the greatest sin of the church is that it regularly withholds the Gospel from itself." You have only to look around you in the flagging fellowship of believers to see how true this is. *"Preach the Gospel to yourself every day,"* was the advice of one of the great devotional writers. Objectively, the Gospel is "finished"; it can't be *undone* and it need not be *redone*. But subjectively, it must be rehearsed, reenacted in our minds as if we had never heard it at all, and celebrated in a daily paean of praise. Inherently, the Gospel of Jesus Christ is not something we learn once and for all and then move on to higher things. No, no. We will be repeating the "entrance prayer" of the publican in the temple *the day we die*: "God, be merciful to me, *the sinner.*" Then, with the very next gasping breath, we may sing, "Thanks be unto God, who always leads us in triumph in Christ."

In short, we should daily, by the grace and power of God and on the foundation of the revelation of His Word, *"reinvent the wheel."* We must discover the Gospel all over again for ourselves every day.

"Tell me the story of Jesus, Write on my heart every word; Tell me the story most precious, Sweetest that ever was heard."

Since Jesus and His Cross are the centerpieces of Heaven, God won't mind us throwing the arms of faith around those pillars again each morning. Begin your Quiet Time with a rehearsal of the glorious Gospel of the Son of God, and God will "tune your heart to sing His praise" all day long.

The "coordination of the Spirit," the miracle "booking" of God, is absolutely amazing when a believer walks in the Spirit. Just today, in my early morning Quiet Time with Him, I found a long paragraph in my devotional reading that practically echoes the idea of this vignette. I am going to juggle a few sentences and then repeat the paragraph here. "The revelation of the Gospel of Christ, the gospel of faith, is the key revelation that surmounts all other visions and prophecies. There is no other way to grasp the things of the Spirit except by direct revelation, and this is as true for ordinary people today as it was for the Biblical prophets and apostles. Saying prayers, going to church, even reading the Bible are not enough. There must be direct, personal, experiential contact with the living God. Yes, the Bible is God's Word; but a person can study the Bible all his life and never hear from God. How pathetic it is to see fine human minds poking and prodding the Scriptures to try and force some meaning out of them, when the fact is that God's Word can only be understood by hearing God speak it all over again into your very own heart, so that the Word becomes as new and as fresh as the day it was first heard and written down. The apostles were great because they were the first to be told the mystery of the Gospel. But doesn't every Christian today have the same experience of God's grace as they did? Every Christian receives a personal revelation of the Gospel directly from

Christ. Every Christian meets Jesus personally, walks with Him and talks with Him, and the result is spectacularly life-changing." Christian, you must prioritize this Gospel-based revelation from God, this experience of hearing His voice, and the resulting relationship with Him – every day.

As usual, a last word of caution is needed. The Gospel is a "two-edged sword." "The Word of God is living and active, and *sharper than any two-edged sword.*" Its narrow blade (truth is always narrow) cuts to the quick. It is incisive and surgical, and its power slices to the core of our character. When we are walking in the Spirit, the very Presence of the Spirit enables us to joyfully take the "cut," knowing that "this is what it's all about." But when we come to the Closet corrupt and cold, character-twisted and calculating, the Word pierces us like the cold steel of an enemy warrior. This is what Glyn Evans meant when he described God as our "beloved Adversary." When we are out of sync because of selfishness and sin, the Word is *surgical and/or medicinal.* "Physician, heal thyself." Take the thrust of the Sword, and let it alert and repair you. Take the medicine, which tastes extremely bitter at the moment of ingestion. It may be His forced feeding, like a loving parent feeding bad-tasting medicine to an ailing child.

Forget the bitter taste of the moment, anticipate the healing, and look for the "nevertheless, afterward" (Hebrews 12:11). To be able to demonstrate "the peaceable fruit of righteousness" for *your good, His glory,* and *the eternal gratification of multitudes of others,* will be reward enough for getting things right when you grip the door-knob into the Prayer Closet.

Chapter 7

THE PRIORITY OF PRAYER

Luke 11:1-4; 9-13:
"And it came to pass, that, as Jesus was praying in a certain place, when he ceased, one of his disciples said unto him, Lord, teach us to pray, as John also taught his disciples. And he said unto them, When ye pray, say, our Father, which art in heaven, Hallowed be thy name. Thy kingdom come. Thy will be done, as in heaven, so in earth. Give us day by day our daily bread. And forgive us our sins, for we also forgive every one that is indebted to us. And lead us not into temptation; but deliver us from evil.

And I say unto you, Ask, and it shall be given you; seek, and ye shall find; knock; and it shall be opened unto you. For every one that asketh receiveth; and he that seeketh findeth; and to him that knocketh it shall be opened. If a son shall ask bread of any of you that is a father, will he give him a stone? Or if he ask a fish, will he for a fish give him a serpent? Or if he shall ask an egg, will he offer him a scorpion? If ye then, being evil, know how to give good gifts unto your children, how much more shall your heavenly Father give the Holy Spirit to them that ask him?"

In 1818, James Montgomery, an intensely devotional Christian leader, wrote these often-repeated wonderful words:

> "Prayer is the soul's sincere desire, Hidden or expressed;
> The motion of a hidden fire, That trembles in the breast.
> Prayer is the Christian's vital breath, The Christian's native air,
> His watchword at the gate of death, And he enters Heaven with prayer."

I see these poetic lines as some of the most insightful words ever written about prayer by a mere mortal man.

I also regard the verses of our text for this message as the greatest single passage about prayer in the entire Bible. I have deliberately omitted the middle portion of this text (verses 5-8), not because it is less significant, but because those are so significant that they deserve to be treated alone. Lest that be misunderstood, let me show how these verses all fit together to constitute Jesus' great teaching on prayer. Here is a simple outline that integrates the entire passage, including the dynamic cameo parable of verses five through eight.

I. A MODEL for prayer, 11:1-4
A. Three petitions center on God and His glory, vs 2
B. Three petitions center on man and his needs, vss 3-4

II. MOTIVATIONS for Prayer, 11:5:13
A. Seen in the little parable, 5-8
B. Seen in some large promises, 9-13

In the outline we will use for this study, we will be much more extensive in treating the many ideas of this great passage about prayer.

I. The INFLUENCE of Prayer, vs. 1

The passage opens with a powerful testimony of the influence of prayer. "As Jesus was praying in a certain place, when he ceased, one of His disciples said unto Him, Lord, teach us to pray, as John also taught His disciples." Every practicing Christian knows something of the delights and the dynamic of prayer. "The effectual, fervent prayer of a righteous man avails much," James wrote (5:16). Prayer is probably the greatest untapped resource on planet earth. Tennyson wrote that "more things are wrought by prayer than this world dreams of," and this is one of the great understatements of history. However, at this point, I am not referring so much to the power of prayer as to the unplanned influence of the person who models a life of prayer. It is obvious from the first verse of our text that Jesus taught by example before He taught by exhortation. With regard to prayer, His practice spoke as clearly as His proclamation.

The influence of prayer is seen in our story, first, in the practice of Jesus. It was "as Jesus was praying in a certain place" that "one of His disciples" approached him with a request about prayer. James Stewart, the great pastor and New Testament scholar of Edinburgh, once said that "the greatest argument for prayer ever known to man is to see the praying Christ on His knees." Our text is located in the Gospel of Luke. The Gospel of Luke is the Gospel that highlights the full and true humanity of Jesus. It shows Him functioning as true and dependent man. You see, Jesus didn't only come from Heaven to reveal what God is like, He came to reveal to us what man should be like. It is no mere coincidence that Luke shows Jesus at prayer more often than any of the other Gospels. He prayed before every "crucial" event in His Life (and Death). Indeed, He is still "dressed out as a

Man" in Heaven today—and He is still praying for us continually there. What would happen if Christians took the cue of His influence to pray, and followed His practice of prayer?

The influence of prayer is seen in our story in a second person and in his teachings about prayer. It is seen, secondly, in the precepts of John the Baptist. Jesus called John "the greatest man born of woman." It is the consistent testimony of Scripture that the great people are those who happily acknowledge their absolute dependence upon the living God, and practice that dependence through regular prayer. John the Baptist was an incredibly powerful man, and his power is attributable to his "desert walk" with God in prayer. The disciple of Jesus who made his request of Jesus about prayer also appealed to the influence of John the Baptist upon him and his request when he said, "Lord, teach us to pray, as John also taught his disciples."

II. Our IGNORANCE of Prayer, vs 1b

The second thing exposed by the text is the disciple's (any disciple's) *ignorance* of prayer. Note the dimensions of the disciple's proposal as he approached Jesus. He had a favor to ask, and he came to the Right Person. An old song says, "Tell it to Jesus, tell it to Jesus, He is a Friend who is well known." This disciple came to Jesus and addressed Him as "Lord." Before He can truly be your Teacher, He must first be your Lord. In John 13:13-14, Jesus made a subtle distinction for His disciples. He said, "You call me Master (Teacher) and Lord: an you are correct, for so I am." But then He added a statement that contained a subtle change of order in the titles, "If I then, your Lord and Master (Teacher)...." The disciples' order of experience with Jesus was this: they had met Him as Teacher first, then the Holy Spirit implanted in them the growing awareness and conviction that this "teacher" is the absolute Lord of the universe.

Then this disciple made the right petition. "Lord, teach us to pray." No disciple of Christ feels himself to be intelligent enough about prayer, or involved enough in the practice of it. Why do we not simply follow the example of Jesus—and pray? Why do we not largely abandon the academics of prayer and engage in the activity of prayer? Some of the biggest answers to prayer and about prayer will come as we "bow our knees before the Father of our Lord Jesus Christ"!

The disciple's request also allowed Jesus to give us the right pattern for our praying, but we will hold that until the next point.

III. His INSTRUCTIONS about prayer, vss. 2-4

Thank God for the disciple's request, because it became the occasion for Jesus to give us the great "Lord's Prayer," as we call it. Here, He provided some of His greatest *instructions* about prayer. He gave us a "model," or a pattern, for our prayers. Note the factors in His instructions.

First, He said, "When you pray, say, ..." Note that Jesus did not say, "if you pray." It is as if Heaven assumes that every man will be needy enough, intelligent enough, and wise enough, to pray. Especially is this true of every twice-born child of God. When a sinner is born again, the Holy Spirit, the Divine Physician who brings the baby to birth, seems to "slap the baby on the backside", which means, Pray without ceasing! Prayer is so automatic and inevitable for a new Christian that he would have to backslide to stop praying! When he was brought to birth in the Family of God, he instantly had a "prayer-instinct" planted into him by the Holy Spirit, just as a newborn baby has planted in it a sucking instinct which reveals it's need for food. "You have received the Spirit of adoption, whereby we cry, Abba (the child's earliest word for his father, equivalent to our 'Dada'), Father." Note that Jesus also said, "When you pray, say." Christians have had a lot of discussion, some of it heated, on the question, "Did Jesus mean that we should actually speak the exact words of this prayer, or should we simply study it as a kind of small-scale model for all of our praying. I simply don't know, but I do occasionally "say" the exact words of this prayer. More significantly, I let the words of this prayer "shape" the general contours of my prayers. What can we learn from this "model" that will help us to pray?

Note first that all the pronouns that refer to us in this prayer are plural. It is "Our Father," not "my Father." It is "give us...," not, "give me." It is "my daily bread," not merely "our daily bread." It is "forgive us," not merely "forgive me." It is "we also forgive," not merely "I forgive." It is "lead us," not merely "lead me." You see, Jesus is forcing us by His model to pray "in the plural." Again and again, Jesus stressed the need for each of us born-agains to move beyond personal piety to a consuming concern for our brothers and sisters in our community and in the world-wide community of true believers in Christ. The reason for this emphasis? Self-absorption is a major problem in any relationship! Jesus Christ apparently intends for us to be always conscious of our place and part in His larger Family, and never to forget it! We are to be "others-conscious" as we pray, seeking the welfare of others and not just our own interests. Philippians 2:4 says, "Look not every man (merely) on his own things, but every man also on the things of others." Friends, the use of all of the plurals in the prayer is no accident, and God is very, very serious about turning each of His born-again children into an "inside-out" person.

Note again that the first two words of the prayer are, "Our Father." Specifically, the word "Our" which opens the prayer indicates that we must pray as members of a fellowship, and the following word, "Father," indicates that we must pray as members of a Family, the "forever family" of God. Question: is your "life-house" more like a house of mirrors (in which you essentially see only yourself) or more like a house of windows (from which you also see others)? Is your life more like a purse (in which you hoard things for your own use), or more like a pipeline? Remember, when water pours through a pipe, it gets the pipe wet, but the destination of the water is not the pipe—it is flowing somewhere else! Is your life more like an expenditure (an expenditure is final, with little return, and it means a reduction of resources) or an investment (never final as long as the investment is kept current, has steady returns, and means an increase of resources).

Let me quote a long, imaginative section from a splendid book entitled <u>The Inner Life of the Believer</u>, by Sherwood Wirt.

In an effort to address the problem, I have prepared a dialogue between a young Christian, not too well grounded, and his heavenly Father. It is not intended to be taken too seriously, from a theological perspective, but it does seek to illustrate why God does not respond with alacrity to some of our batterings on the heavenly gates. I will have a final comment at the close. "Well, Father." "Yes, son." "I thought I'd better check in with You. I'm kind of waiting for an answer." "From me?" "Who else? I mean, that's it, isn't it? If You say go..." "What do you want?" "I want to be filled with Your Spirit." "Are you sure of this?" "You bet. I want it all—the baptism, the anointing, the indwelling, the gifts, the fruit, the filling, the whole package." "And?" "Well, it's like the ball is

The Daily Quiet Time

in Your court, sort of. Everything's set." "How is everything set?" "Well, You know. I prayed and humbled myself." [My note: Here is the usual "argument" of Christians—as if God were tied and gagged because we prayed; as if He is obligated to us—because "I prayed about it." Prayer is not God's carte blanche to us, but our means of adjustment to Him! It is more basking than asking!] "How did you humble yourself?" "Well, I thought I did. And I fasted." "One meal." "Look, Father, I'm serious. I'm waiting on you." "And I am waiting on you." "Do you have to? After all, You made me. You know I'm young and full of life. I want to see some action. I've watched what happens when You pour Your Spirit into some other guys. It's really neat. I can't wait to get in on it." "So you can't wait." "No. Why should I? What's the point of waiting? I don't have forever, Lord." "But I do." "That's fine for You, Father. What about the people who are dying every day and going to hell?" "You have plans?"

Are we beginning to see the implications of this Model Prayer?

Now, let's examine the substance of the prayer. After the "Our Father" opening, the prayer identifies Him further, "Our Father which art in Heaven." The word "Father" points out His nearness and His intimacy with us, but the next phrase points out His transcendence and His sovereignty. So our prayers must be marked by a balanced awareness of His tenderness and His transcendence.

This balance came home to me in a simple household incident one morning years ago. I was approaching a home to make a call. A young puppy was lying on the porch. When I turned up the walk to reach the home, the puppy arose and came down the steps, tail wagging moderately. When it reached the sidewalk, it turned sideways and continued its approach to me in that manner, taking sideways steps. Its tail was as close to me as its head! What was the puppy saying? Basically, "The call is yours, sir. If you beckon me forward, I will rush to meet you, but if you show any sign of disfavor, I'm out of here in respectful deference to you." In respectful deference to You (not in our usual dictatorial expectation) is the way we as dependent children should approach God. This is not a slavish rule, just one that honors His Godhood. True, God is "our Father", but it is equally important to remember that our Father is GOD.

After the introductory address, the prayer contains six petitions. Analyzing them carefully is a spiritual education! The six petitions are equally divided into two parts, and each part has three petitions. The first three petitions center on God, and the last three center on man. The order is very important, and reveals plainly why so many of our prayers are unanswered. When we begin the prayer with our needs, in total disregard for the Person, purposes and glory of God, we are guaranteed to receive a "cold shoulder" from Him. Many of our prayers are unanswered because we "ask amiss, that we may consume the benefit received upon our own lusts" (James 4:3).

Note the three petitions that center on God and His glory. "Hallowed (recognized as holy) be Thy Name (the Name represents the Person), Thy kingdom come, Thy will be done, as in heaven, so in earth." These three petitions need one careful item of interpretation. The phrase, "as in heaven, so in earth," actually qualifies and applies to all three petitions, not merely to the last one (as in the King James Version). You see, in a Greek text, there are no punctuation marks, so one major task of any translator is to decide what punctuation should be used to convey the intended meaning of the text, and where that punctuation should occur. Did you know that, many years ago, an entire session of the British Parliament was convened to debate the placement of the comma which occurs in the King James Bible after the phrase, "Thy will be done." This issue is far more important than we may think (most Christians have never thought of this at all). If the comma is omitted, the qualifying clause, "as in Heaven, so in earth," applies only to the preceding phrase, "Thy will be done." But if the comma is included, the qualifying phrase applies to all three of the previous appeals. Of course, the comma should be included, as it is in my King James Version of the Bible. The qualifying phrase applies to all three petitions, not just to the last one. So it would be wise for the reader to include the qualifying phrase with each of the three appeals. They would look like this:

> "Hallowed be Thy Name—as in heaven, so in earth."
> "Thy kingdom come—as in heaven, so in earth."
> "Thy will be done—as in heaven, so in earth."

The qualifying clause in each case asks that God may be honored on earth exactly the way He is already fully honored, adored and glorified in Heaven. So, based on these insights, let's establish another principle for living the Christian life. One of the very best ways to live the Christian Life is to look up into Heaven, find out what is going on there, and ask God to reproduce it in and through us right here on earth! If this were to happen, God's Person would be fully acknowledged and honored, God's pre-eminence would be practiced, and God's purpose would be fulfilled—in the very community where each of us lives!

Now, let's turn to the three petitions that center on man and his needs. The three petitions have to do with daily provision, daily pardon, and daily protection, the three all-inclusive categories of man's needs. "Give us this day our daily bread"—the appeal for daily provision. Give attention to two things in this appeal. First, it strongly suggests when we are to pray this prayer each day. It simply wouldn't be sensible to climb into bed at night and ask God for bread for that day—the day is already past! No, this prayer is rigged to the earliest part of the day, one of the "first things" that are to be dedicated to God in our lives. We pray for daily provision when we are facing the day, not when its necessities and responsibilities are behind us. Secondly, we are to pray for "our daily bread," not for our daily "cake"! People like us in western (American) culture are so spoiled with benefits that we regard everything we have as daily bread, but the rest of the world would regard those same benefits as daily cake. That is, most of what we have could be accurately defined as luxuries ("cake"), not necessities ("bread"). But, fellow Christians in America, we had better draw the distinction now, because it is likely that God will force a tightening of our belts so we will be reminded of the Source of all that we have (whether luxuries or necessities)! And remember that He has only committed Himself to giving us daily bread, not daily cake!

"And forgive us our sins; for we also forgive every one that is indebted to us." Note the order of these first two man-centered petitions. First, material blessings ("daily bread"), then spiritual blessing (forgiveness of our sins). Why this order? Because a man who is starving to death likely will not hear a presentation of the Gospel until he has food to eat. Man was a physical creature with physical necessities before he became aware that he also had spiritual needs as well. So the appeal for physical blessings comes first in Jesus' model prayer.

However, we must not misunderstand the order here, and deduce that man's spiritual needs are less important or not important at all. Forgiveness of sin is an eternally pressing need! In fact, it is an ever-pressing need hour-by-hour! There is nothing in a sinner's life more critical than forgiveness of sin, and there is nothing that brings greater relief and release than the full assurance that all of your sins are forgiven, blotted out, removed from the record, and dismissed forever! God's full forgiveness secures all of these benefits, and they are received in the very moment of "repentance toward God and faith in the Lord Jesus Christ" (Acts 20:21) on the part of the sinner.

Note too that Jesus acknowledges the seriousness of sin when He identifies it as a "debt," a debt owed and pledged to God by our sins. Every sin you have ever committed constitutes an "IOU" written out, signed, and extended to God. These recorded IOUs of God's broken law have accumulated on God's "office desk" and stand as an inviolable record "against" you (Colossians 2:15-16). The creditors who demand payment for these IOUs of sin are the Holiness of God, the Law of God, and the Justice of God. The rule is this: either your sins will be pardoned in Christ on the just basis of His full payment for them on Calvary, or your sins will be punished in hell, and the punishment will be meted out upon the guilty party—and he remains guilty on the basis of the continuing commitment of sin, even after he enters hell, so the debt of sin continues to be paid forever. Serious, serious issues, indeed! So forgiveness of sins is a crucially urgent matter, and Jesus taught us to pray expectantly and faithfully for it.

Before we leave the forgiveness petition, we must also face the proviso that He attached to our forgiveness. "Forgive us our sins; for we also forgive every one that is indebted to us." The reason for this is simple: the size of our "output" of forgiveness will determine the size of our "intake" of forgiveness. If we willfully refuse the output of our own forgiveness to others, we are dictating to God that He should restrict His offer and our intake of Divine forgiveness. If we refuse to forgive others for their relatively small sins against us, how can we expect God to forgive our incredibly big sins against Him?

Now, the third of the man-centered petitions: "And lead us not into temptation, but deliver us from evil." If this prayer refers to the matter of temptation to sin, the prayer is completely unnecessary, because we already have in the Bible a clear promise that "God cannot be tempted with evil, neither does He tempt any man" (James 1:13). You see, the same Greek word (*peirasmos*) may be translated either by the word "temptation" or the word "trial(s)". In fact, it is translated by both words in the Bible. In the first case, it refers to enticement to sin, but in the second case, it refers to circumstantial (not moral) evil, and should be translated "trials." In the Model Prayer, the appeal to God to "not lead us into temptation" is an appeal to God to protect us from evil circumstances or dangerous situations, and it is likely that the "deliver us from evil" plea also has to do with evil circumstance. The Book of Job in the Old Testament is an exploration of the power and agony of being engulfed by evil circumstances. Here, Jesus teaches us to ask "our Father" for protection from such evil power and the agony that attends its exercise in our lives.

Let me remind you (and myself) of the exact nature of the three man-centered appeals; they are requests for daily provision or supply, for daily pardon of sin, and for daily protection from evil situations. So the appeals of the prayer direct our attention to God first, then to ourselves and our needs. Now, we will skip over the little parable recorded in verses 5 through 8 (I have written another study on the parable) and go to the final teachings of Jesus on prayer recorded in this passage.

IV. The IMPACT of Prayer, verses 9-12

In verses nine through twelve, Jesus informs us of the impact of prayer. In verses nine and ten, He said, "And I say unto you, Ask, and it shall be given you; seek, and ye shall find; knock, and it shall be opened unto you. For every one that asketh receiveth; and he that seeketh findeth; and to him that knocketh, it shall be opened." These verses look easy and innocent, but as usual, there is much, much more here than meets the eye of the too-casual reader. Note that the first letters of the three key verbs, "ask", "seek", and "find", form the letters of the first word in the succession, "A-S-K." This is simply an easy way to remember the simplicity of prayer. I am convinced that these three verbs refer to three different levels of prayer, and the text certainly gives strong support to this view.

The word "ask" refers to the simplest and easiest level of prayer. It refers to the presenting of a simple petition to God. Jesus said, "Your Father knows such things as you have need of, before you ask." But He still insists that we ask, in order to bring us to Him—because we need Him more than we need anything He can give us. But the second word, "seek," reveals that this is a more difficult level of prayer, because there is now a search between the one praying and the answer to his prayer. So the difficulty has intensified. Then, the third word, "knock." Ah, now there is a solid barrier, a door, between the one praying and the blessing he seeks. So these requests increase in the difficulty that is encountered at each new level.

There is another subtlety of interpretation in these "simple" statements. In the first level (vss 9, 10), the words "ask" and "receive" are both present-tense verbs. The same is true of "seek" and "find" (vss 9, 10) But though the third appeal, "knock," is also present-tense(vss 9, 10), the words, "and it shall be opened unto you" (vss 9b, 10b) is future tense. Furthermore, the one asking and the one receiving in the first case, is the same person. In the second case, the one seeking and the one finding are also the same person. But in the third case, the one knocking and the one opening the door are not the same person. The one who knocks is one person, while the one opening the door is a different person altogether. So it is evident that Jesus is teaching us about three different levels of prayer here. Also, the future tense, "it shall be opened unto you," indicates that in the third level, the one praying may be forced to wait a long time for the answer, which again shows the more difficult level of prayer. I personally believe that He is talking in the third case about praying for others, particularly for lost people, and that prayer may be answered only after a long struggle over a lost man's soul.

To summarize, the first level of prayer calls simply for petition to be made ("ask"), the second level intensifies the difficulty and calls for persistence on the part of the one praying, persistence in searching for the answer ("seek"), and the third level is the hardest of all, calling for extended perseverance to be practiced ("knock")—until "the door is opened unto you."

The next verses, verses 11 and 12, are some of the most searching and insightful verses on prayer in the entire Bible. Notice that Jesus enforces His family reference here. He begins, "If a son...of any of you that is a father." Here He appeals to what we can generally know about a father-son relationship. But He deliberately causes us to think of a most unusual situation between father and son. In verse 11, He said, "If a son shall ask bread of any of you who is a father, will the father give him a stone?" This son is apparently hungry, and he makes a normal request of his father for food, which is something necessary, something beneficial, something nutritional. In that case, Jesus asked, would his father give him a rock instead of the bread he requested? Here, He apparently expects us to "see through" the question. The son asks for bread, something useful and necessary; instead the father gives him something worthless. He could suck on a rock all day long and wouldn't extract any food value out of it. So what prayer-principle is Jesus constructing? Here it is: God will never (ever) in answer to your prayers give you something that is worthless to you and His purpose for you—from His viewpoint! So He very plainly tells us why many of our prayers will not or cannot be answered.

Then He changes the illustration to an even more ridiculous extreme—again to present a crucial point about prayer. In verse 11b, He said, "Or if he (the son) ask a fish, will he (the father) instead of a fish give him a serpent?" Here, the word "serpent" is major emphasis in the Greek text, emphasizing that this is an outlandish idea. In verse 12, Jesus created a similar possibility, thus enforcing His idea: "Or if he (the son) shall ask an egg, will he (the father) offer him a scorpion?" What a strange scenario! What does it mean? Well, in the preceding paragraph, we saw the father offering something worthless to his son when he needed something good and wholesome and essential. But here, when the son makes his request for food, the father gives him instead something that is absolutely dangerous! Both serpent and scorpion carry dangerous poisons and can be very painful or deadly in administering their venom. So again we must ask, what prayer-principle is Jesus presenting here? Here it is: God will never (ever) in answer to your prayers give you something that is dangerous to you and His purpose for you—from His standpoint! However, if we pause and examine His Word, we would find that many things people request of God in prayer are, in fact, both worthless and dangerous to the one praying and to God's purpose for him—from God's viewpoint. So we must be very careful to learn all of the allowable, advisable, and prohibited, things we may or may not pray for. Otherwise, we are asking God for things that He very clearly has said He will not give us.

This great passage on prayer closes with a power-packed statement, a statement in which Jesus presents an *ad hominem* argument, that is, He begins with the best we can see in men and argues upward to what we can deduce about God. "If you then, being evil, know how to give good gifts unto your children; how much more shall your Heavenly Father give the Holy Spirit to them that ask Him?" This verse deserves much meditation, study and dependence upon the Holy Spirit to even begin to see the vast riches that are here. I have several booklets in my library entitled, <u>None But the Hungry Heart,</u> and each is an attempt to show that God has deliberately hidden incredible riches in the deep mine of His Word so that, while a casual reader may find good truths, only the person hungry enough to go deep and mine the "mother lode" will find these incredible riches hidden there. This verse is another case in point.

Note that Jesus establishes that all of His readers and listeners are "evil," that is, that all of us are sinners. The only exception to this absolute rule in the human race is Jesus Himself, who was without sin. Furthermore, the word "evil" in the Greek text carries major emphasis, meaning, "very evil." If people are honest and have really looked into the depths of their hearts, they would find no room to argue with Him. We are indeed "evil"! To the degree to which we see and admit that, to that very degree, the message of Christ is indeed a Gospel, or Good News, to each of us as sinners.

Then, having declared that we are evil, He establishes that even evil sinners do know how to give good gifts to their children. Again, we must pause at the words of the text. Look at the word "good", for example. The Greek language has two common words that are often or usually translated by our word "good," but the two words have variations of meaning. One is the Greek word *kalos*, which basically means "good in appearance, attractive, winsome," or "beautiful" to the senses. This is the word Jesus used when He described the act of the woman who poured a flask of perfume on His head. "She has done a beautiful thing to Me," He declared, using the word *kalos*. But that is not the word that is used in our text. The word here is *agathos*, which means "inwardly, intrinsically, inherently good." This is the word that would be used for a gift that is "useful, beneficial, advantageous" to the recipient. Jesus said that even sinners know how to give very good, practical, useful, beneficial, advantageous gifts to their own children, and He was certainly right. Then He added one of His own favorite phrases to make His point. "How much more," He said, "How much more (than the goodness of sinners can reveal) shall your Heavenly Father (Who is Himself perfectly "good" in every way) give –what? "The Holy Spirit to them that ask Him?" What a verse! What an assurance! The words, "How much more," were three of Jesus' favorite words. But again, there is more here than meets the too-casual eye.

Remember that these words were spoken before the Day of Pentecost, which marked the coming of the Holy Spirit in the full release of redemptive power. Today, no Christian has to "ask" for the Holy Spirit. Indeed, if the Holy Spirit is not in a person, that person is not born again. "If any man have not the Spirit of Christ, he is none of His" (Romans 8:9). Again and again, we are told that the Spirit of God, the Spirit of adoption, lives within a believer to give assurance to him that he is a "child of God." Today, we don't ask for the Holy Spirit since He is already within us who are born again, but it is necessary for each of us to live in total submission to Him to experience and enjoy His control, His fullness, His power, His fruitfulness, in our lives. You see, the Holy Spirit may live in us and still be "grieved" (Ephesians 4:30) and "quenched" (I Thessalonians 5:19); but when we live in cooperative faith in Him, He fills us with His own grace and power.

Another subtlety in the text: Note how Jesus identifies the Gift that the Heavenly Father "gives to them that ask Him." "How much more shall your Heavenly Father give the Holy Spirit to them that ask Him"—as if to declare that the Holy Spirit is the best of all the "good gifts" God gives to His children. And, indeed, He is! At this point, we may learn a vast lifetime lesson of exceeding value to God's child. You see, this same verse (verse 13) is also recorded in Matthew 7:11, but with one very significant variation. Except for one tiny phrase, Luke 11:13 and Matthew 7:11 are exactly the same. Luke 11:13 closes with these words: "... how much more shall your Heavenly Father give the *Holy Spirit* to them that ask Him." Matthew 7:11 says, "... how much more shall your Heavenly Father give *good things* to them that ask Him." In both of these quotes, the italics are mine. They show the slight (!) variation in the two verses. What does this mean? It means that the Holy Spirit is equivalent to all truly good things in the economy of God and for the child of God! We must be sure to understand this. The Holy Spirit is a "translatable Person," a "negotiable commodity" if we know how to "convert" Him according to our needs and His purpose. Is this not what the title "I Am" means about God? I Am – what? This allows us to fill in the amount of any legitimate need (legitimate from God's perspective) and receive Him as our Supply. The same is true of the Holy Spirit, and this is substantiated in many Scripture passages.

Some years ago when I was a pastor in another state, a church member approached me one day in distress and requested, "Please pray that God will give me peace." Without any thought of being impolite or insensitive, I asked, "Are you sure you are saved?" She answered, "Yes! I know that I am saved!" I said, "Then I cannot pray that prayer for you." Shocked, she said, "You can't ask God to give me peace?" "No, I can't; you see, if you are saved, you already have all the peace you need—but apparently you don't know how to appropriate what you have." Then I explained to her, "God never intends to give us His blessings or gifts independently of Himself. We need Him far more than we need anything He might give us. Furthermore, He has fixed everything so that when we get Him, we get all we need. Colossians 2:10 says, 'We are complete in Him,' but most Christians have never been taught how to exploit such truths for their own good and His greater glory. Let me ask you a simple question. In your personal experience, where is the Holy Spirit right now?" "He is inside of me," she answered. I said, "Doesn't the Bible say that 'the fruit of the Spirit is love, joy, peace, . . .'? If He dwells in you, then you already have all that He is and all that He is able and willing to be in you." "Then what should I do? How do I pray?" "Simply ask Him to BE your peace; that is, appropriate the Gift by translating the Peaceful Giver! In fact, ask Him to be your love, and your joy, etc. Ask the Holy Spirit to be your very disposition! HE IS EQUIVALENT TO ALL 'GOOD THINGS' FOR A CHRISTIAN; JUST TRANSLATE HIM INTO WHAT YOU NEED (if the 'need' agrees with God's viewpoint)."

The Priority of Prayer

Near the end of her long life and her long reign as Queen of England (64 years), Queen Victoria visited Sheffield to open the gates of the new town hall of that city. She was so feeble that it was thought best that she not leave her carriage, so hidden electrical wires were fastened to a golden key fitting into the lock, which she could turn as she sat in her carriage. She operated the device and turned the key, and some distance away, slowly, surely, the gates of the Town Hall opened. We have a key like that which opens the door between us and God. We cannot see the wires which connect the golden key of prayer with Heaven's gate, but a voice which we trust says to us, "Turn the key; turn the golden key."

Chapter 8

THE CHRISTIAN LIFE AND PRAYER

Luke 18:1: *"At all times men ought to pray and not to lose heart."*

To live physical life at its best, human beings need these basics, these minimal things: proper food, proper air, proper rest, and proper exercise. In the spiritual realm, there is a corresponding reality to each of these needs. The "spiritual man" (I Corinthians 2:14) needs a daily balanced diet of the Word of God, daily and continuous communion with God in prayer, the steady spiritual rest of abiding in Christ and being carried by Him from within, and the consistent outward exercises of true Christian action.

These necessities must be kept in reasonable balance in the growing Christian's life. For example, a believer who is strong in the Word of God but weak in prayer is like a skeleton with no flesh on it. But the believer who is heavy in prayer but weak in the Word of God is like a jellyfish—all meat and no skeleton. Balance is essential in all of the disciplines mentioned above.

In this study, we will explore in a very simple manner the theme of "Prayer and the Christian Life." In doing so, I will use the cue that is found in a couplet in Rudyard Kipling's book, Just So Stories.

"I keep six serving men, They taught me all I knew;
Their names are What, Where, When, How, Why and Who."

In the world of journalism, these questions are often referred to as "the editorial questions," or "the six editorial friends." I will let these questions provide the structure for this study.

I. WHAT IS PRAYER?

The first question we will ask and seek to answer about prayer is, "What is it?" Very simply, prayer has been defined as "the talking side of your relationship with God." Or, to be a bit more accurate and adequate, it is the communicating side of your relationship with God. In a powerful and helpful passage, Paul indicates the distinction between mere audible "talking" and true prayer when he indicated that sometimes prayer cannot be articulated; it rather takes the form of "groanings which cannot be articulated" (Romans 8:26). But prayer still may be defined as talking with God.

As to the forms of prayer, we want to mention at least these categories: Adoration (expressions of awareness and appreciation for Who God is); Confession (awareness and admission of our depravity and our dependence upon God); Thanksgiving (expressions of gratitude for all that God has done in us, for us, and among us); and Intercession (taking a position of identification with other people and their needs, and acting as their representative, taking their needs and interest before God).

It is vital to realize this principle: Prayer does not need *explanation* as much as it needs *expression;* prayer does not need *argument* as much as it needs *demonstration;* prayer doesn't need *proof* as much as it needs *practice.* Both *theology* and *"knee-ology"* are needed in understanding and implementing prayer in your life.

Prayer is a time exposure to God. Prayer is more basking in God than it is asking of God. One wise saint said, "Prayer is Son-bathing, and it certainly makes you look different, both in inner satisfaction and in outward action." Note her word, "look", in that sentence. This is true subjectively for the praying Christian; that is, prayer conditions the things you look at and your reasons for looking, and it is also true objectively; that is, prayer determines the result of your looking. My lifetime motto verse expresses these truths: "But we all, beholding as in a mirror the glory of the Lord Jesus, are being transformed into the same image as the One we are beholding, and this transformation progresses from one stage of glory to the next higher stage of glory, and this is the work of the Spirit of the Lord," (my arrangement of 2 Cors 3:18).

Prayer is seed sown on the heart of God. Again, "he who sows sparingly shall reap also sparingly, but he who sows bountifully shall reap also bountifully" (II Corinthians 9:6). You see, when prayers are sown as seeds on God's heart, the praying believer will discover that the *harvest* is as big and boundless as the promises and purposes of God. Thus, every believer should begin each morning making a prayer appeal based on the opening words of Jesus in the great parable of the sower: "Behold, a sower went forth to sow." See your prayers as spiritual seeds falling into the compassionate heart of your loving Father, and watch for the harvest!

II. WHO MAY PRAY?

The second question in our study is, "Who may pray?" Nowhere in the Bible is prayer offered indiscriminately as an exercise that may be productively indulged by all men. Biblically, prayer is the privilege of the people of God, of the child of God. By that I mean that it belongs by right of having been "born from above," "born again," born spiritually with a real a revolutionary birth that has placed the once-sinner, now-saint, into the Forever Family of God.

Jesus said to His followers, "When you pray, say, 'Our Father'." The word "our" means that we are to pray as members of a vast fellowship of believers, and the word "Father" means that we are to pray as members of a vast family. So every prayer should be marked by the awareness of all other members of the fellowship and all other members of the Family. This proves to be a mighty blow against our sinful isolationism and individualism, and a powerful aid in building a fellowship-consciousness and a Family-consciousness in all believers. When this occurs, there will be no superiority or inferiority among the people of God, and there will be no competition among Christians (read and study II Corinthians 10:12 carefully). I would prefer to remain completely positive in this discussion of prayer, and not to wander off into assessments of the problems that are often engineered by careless thoughts, words and actions in the Body of Christ with regard to its "fellowship".

III. WHERE SHOULD WE PRAY?

In our study of prayer, the third question is, "Where should we pray?" The answer is that there is, in fact, *no* place where prayer may not be made. From Jonah in the whale (Jonah 2), to Paul and Silas in the jail (Acts 16), human beings may "get the King's ear." Paul wrote to Timothy, "I will that men pray *everywhere.*" (I Timothy 2:8) Of course, this may only mean that Paul is appealing to men everywhere to pray, but it may also mean that men may and should pray anywhere they are. Again, the principle of "the dedicated place" doesn't intend to teach that only that place, only those places, belong to God, but rather that the *one* place devoted to Him sanctifies *all* places to His Person and His purpose.

In Matthew 6:6, Jesus guarded His followers against a public prayer parade for publicity's sake when He said, "*But you* (unlike the hypocrites), *when* you pray (again, assuming that it is supernaturally natural for a born-again person to pray), enter into *your closet*, and when you have *shut your door*, pray to your Father who is in secret; and your Father who sees in secret shall reward you." Every Christian should cultivate the habit as often as possible of corporate prayer, a kind of prayer that has incredible advantages, incredible power, *and is attended by many problems*, but he should guard against the dangers of public, corporate prayer by spending much time and attention on private prayer in his "prayer closet."

My own personal "prayer closet" is a small blue room in our home, very pleasantly decorated and very conducive to meeting with God and shutting out all else. I keep an assortment of prayer aids in this room, including at least two translations of the Word of God, great daily devotional literature, a hymnbook, a prayer list (often comprised of pictures of the people I pray for), and several larger books for devotional reading. Each morning, I choose between maybe twelve items, isolating maybe four of them for use in my "time in the Captain's briefing room." More about the use of these things in a later paragraph under another point.

Any place is a good place to pray.

IV. WHEN SHOULD WE PRAY?

The fourth question is, "When may we pray?" Really, the question should rather be asked, "When should we *not* pray?" There is no time that is a prohibited time as far as prayer is concerned. "There is a time to be born, and a time to die; a time to plant, and a time to pluck up that which is planted; a time to kill, and a time to heal; a time to break down, and a time to build up; a time to weep, and a time to laugh; a time to mourn, and a time to dance; a time to cast away stones, and a time to gather stones together; a time to embrace, and a time to refrain from embracing; a time to get, and a time to lose; a time to keep, and a time to cast away; a time to rend, and a time to sew; a time to keep silence, and a time to speak; a time to love, and a time to hate; a time of war, and a time of peace" (Ecclesiastes 3:1-8). But *any and all times* may be *times for praying.* Indeed, all of the "times" mentioned in that passage might be/could be/should be saturated with prayer. Paul said it inclusively and commandingly when he wrote, "Pray without ceasing" (I Thessalonians 5:17). In the text printed at the head of this study, Jesus said, "Men ought *always* to pray and *not to give up* praying."

Remember that four of the necessities of physical life are food, air, rest, and exercise. You don't expect normally to live one day with food, and you shouldn't allow yourself to live one day without feeding in the Word of God. You go only short intervals without breathing (the air in the statement above), and wouldn't it be wonderful if you should pray as consistently as you breathe?

Though we may and should pray at all times, life will be a lot more than prayer, and the tendency is to crowd out prayer or drift outside the practice of prayer. Thus, the Bible prescribes recommended times for prayer which will set the tone for a spirit of prayer to prevail in the believer all of the time. Psalm 5:3 says, "O Lord, in the morning will I direct my prayer unto You, and will look up." It was recorded of Jesus in Mark 1:35, "And in the morning, rising up a great while before day, He went out, and departed into a solitary place, and there He prayed." Apparently, following the principle of "first fruits", that the devotion of "first things" sanctifies all the rest (example, the tithe, 10 % of one's income, devoted to God, sanctifies the 90 % and indicates that it all belongs to Him and will be used for His purposes, the early practice of prayer each day points the entire day toward God. In Psalm 55:17, the Psalmist said, "Evening, and morning, and at noon will I pray, and cry aloud." This order of the day, which is peculiar to us, honors the Jewish reckoning which declares that a day begins the evening before at sundown. So even this order shows that, by that reckoning, prayers were offered at the beginning of each day. When Jesus said in Matthew 6:5, "When (or 'whenever', showing that the door of prayer is always open) you pray, you are not to be as the hypocrites; for they love to stand and pray in the synagogues and on the street corners, in order to be seen of men," he was not condemning synagogue praying, nor street-corner praying, but merely asking that the motive of our prayers be sifted of man-consciousness so our attention can be turned totally to God. Whenever I pray, I am to give the Sovereign of the universe my undivided attention and affection. In the practice of prayer, consecration is determined by concentration.

V. HOW SHOULD WE PRAY?

Question number five is, "How should we pray?" Anything I might say here is only suggestive, and certainly not exhaustive. I would hope that this point might raise your "creativity bar" so that your tomorrows will be loaded with far more innovative, inventive and creative practices than you have ever dreamed of before now.

Prayer may be said to be comprised of *listening for God and to God, meditating on what has been heard, talking to God, and listening some more* .... It may be regarded as *spiritual reading, sensitive relating,* and *steady repeating and reliving of the lessons learned.* Remember that repetition is the art of life and learning. You know your name simply because someone repeated it to you enough times that you began to repeat it after them. Then it became truly *yours.* The same is true of your telephone number, your street address, etc., etc. All of those "facts" were learned by repetition. A person's claim of "poor memory" is usually an admission of little concentration, little effort, and little intent. Remember, too, our earlier rule that *consecration* is determined by *concentration.* Many people hurriedly abandon any probing thoughts of God—often because of guilt, or embarrassment, or failure, etc., etc. And that person often begins to protest about God to others, again merely an admission of personal deficiency.

How should we pray? Let's begin with *concentration.* Martin Luther, in his quaint and often blunt way, said wistfully, "If only I could pray the way my dog looks at the morsel of food on my plate! All of his thoughts and actions are concentrated on it. At that moment, he is a mix of reverence and desire. Through his reverence for me and fear of me, he won't jump on the table, but because of his desire for the food, he never gives up his longing to possess it." Here is the Christian's balance in prayer, a balance of hunger and humility, a *hunger* that keeps him *in pursuit of God,* but a *humility* that keeps him *from presumption about God.*

How should we pray? Let's chart a possible *course.* I have learned to make it a habit of praying HIM (read the appeal line of the Model Prayer, and then the first three petitions), then praying THEM (both the smaller circle of my own acquaintances, fellow believers, and disciples and disciplers), then praying BOOKS (praying topically over what I am reading), then praying special ASSIGNMENTS, EVENTS and MEETINGS WITH PEOPLE. All of this, and more, is done in my "prayer closet." I say as a caution that we must not forget that the purpose of prayer is not to follow a plan, but to *genuinely commune with a Person*. With regard to the place and the plan, there is not a part of our home which has not been used again and again by my wife and me for special prayer times, or regular prayer times. Sometimes we mute the television to pray over needs, events and people who have been profiled in newscasts, etc. At other times, we pray after hanging up the telephone (and sometimes when still *on* the phone) when we have been made aware of concerns that call for prayer. Often, we pray what I call "sky telegram prayers," brief but at-the-moment and on-the-spot.

I have found that one of the best ways to pray is to hold an open Bible before me, and pray over it, paraphrasing Scripture back to God—with thanksgiving and wonder, application and request, etc. That is, I let the open Bible determine my prayer and supplication, and my worship and celebration. Remember that God has "elevated His Word even above all His Name" (Psalm 138:2). Jesus said, "If you abide in Me, and My words abide in you, you shall ask whatever you wish and it shall be done for you" (John 15:7). So I must agree with God about His Word, and what it means to Him and thus what it should mean to me.

At any time, if I hold Scripture memory cards in my hand, I turn each verse into a *memory* request (asking God to help me memorize it), a *mastery* request (asking God to let this truth master me, and make me a "master of life" through His grace and power) and a *manifestation* request (asking Him to

The Daily Quiet Time

manifest the Truth of this verse *to* me, then *through* me and into my world of relationships and circumstances, today). Actually, these exercises may be used while on trips, while driving across town (using the memory of prayer requests, Scripture verses, relational awareness, etc., etc.), while idling in an easy chair, while flying on an airplane, and even while waiting for a disciple in a restaurant.

How should we pray? Pray with this concept fastened in your heart: It is not the *arithmetic* of our prayers, that is, how *many* prayers we pray; it is not the *rhetoric* of our prayers, that is, how *eloquent* they are; it is not the *geometry* of our prayers, that is, how *long* they are; it is not the *music* of our prayers, that is, how *sweet* they are; it is not the *method* of our prayers, that is, how *orderly*. It is the God-moved, Scripturally-conditioned, *heart in and behind* the prayer that determines its authority and power. "Let us therefore draw near with confidence to the throne of grace" (Hebrews 4:16). It is a "throne", thus, a place of *majesty*, but it is a throne "of *grace*", thus, a place of *mercy*. "Let us draw near"!

My all-time favorite poem is a long running narrative poem from the Elizabethan age, written by the poet-preacher of St. Paul's Cathedral, Dr. John Dunne. Try to work your way through the intricate language of this stanza, and let God stretch your heart.

> "Batter my heart, three Person'd God! For You
> As yet but knock, breathe, shine, and seek to mend;
> That I may rise, and stand, and o'erthrow me, and bend.
> Your force, to break, blow, burn, and make me new.
>
> I am betroth'd unto Your enemy,
> Divorce me, untie, or break that knot again.
> Take me to You, imprison me, for I

Except You enthrall me, never shall be free,
Nor ever chaste, except You ravish me."

Dear Christian, resolve that poem, fragment by fragment, line by line, idea by idea, and do it unhurriedly, meditating until you discover the meaning of his words and ideas, and you have just completed a main course in God's School of Prayer! And if you can't master it to pray it exactly, you can prayer at least like it. "Lord, here am I. I really want to appropriate You to my total life, but I have so little faith. I can't always be sure about how to pray. I am such an ordinary, small-hearted, limited, unspiritual creature. I have tried to open all the doors into my life to You, but there is so much accumulated dirt and rust on the bolts of the doors. You must do it for me. Please break through! Smash the rusty lock! Batter Thou my heart, Thou great Three-Personed God!" May God help us to open all we are and have to His entrance, to His work in us, *and to His exit into the world through us*!

VI. WHY SHOULD WE PRAY?

Our sixth and final question for this study on prayer is, "Why should we pray?" Simply, we must face the fact that there is no advance, no growth, no victory, no power, no productivity, no happy outcome, to the Christian life, without prayer. God cannot work with a prayerless saint! He may drastically work *on* him, upsetting his life incredibly, but He cannot work *with* Him and *through* him. Thus, God's purpose is lost in that Christian's life. That Christian has aborted God's intention and must live with the result forever in a sad loss of reward at the Judgment Seat of Christ and thereafter. Christian, if these words find you in that state, repent immediately and let Him restore you to full favor, full faith, and full fruitfulness. He is more eager to restore you than you are to be restored! You are His child, and though He may discipline you severely, you must remember that "whom He loves, He disciplines."

Why should we pray? We should pray, first, *to relate to God*. God has given you permission, access, and aggressive invitation, to come to Him in prayer. God has suspended great promises and great purposes upon your prayers to Him. God has offered unbelievable victories in His Name and for your sake and the sake of multitudes of other people—in answer to your prayers.

We should pray, also, *to receive from God*. "In everything by prayer and *supplication* (the request for *supply*) with thanksgiving, let your requests be made known to God" (Philippians 4:6). Jesus said, "Ask (present tense continuous action, 'keep on asking'), and you shall receive, seek, and you shall find, knock, and it shall be opened unto you" (Matthew 7:7).

Consult the special study on Luke 11 in which that last verse and its surrounding teaching on prayer are dealt with. In Jeremiah 33:3, God says, "Call unto Me, and I will answer you, and show you great and mighty things, which you don't know." Think carefully about the words "call", "great" and "mighty", and "things which you don't know" (haven't thought about, cannot imagine). That is, there are massive blessings, benefits, victories, advances – treasures – in God's vault in Heaven that you will not discover in this life unless you appeal to Him personally, passionately and purposefully in prayer. When God's "goodie closet" door is cracked for you to look in when you get to Heaven, will you be familiar with any of the "goodies," the riches of His glory and grace, which will be therein – because you prayed during your days on earth, and God flung open the door and said, "Help yourself; these were intended for you, anyway, but they waited on your prayers!!!" If you are on unfamiliar territory at that moment, saved but "barely saved," He might say, "This is what you could have had; why didn't you take the Key that I offered to you and open the lock?"

We should pray, finally, *to redirect our lives* upward (toward Him) and outward (toward others), the two dimensions of the true Christian life—vertical and horizontal, and *to redirect His resources* through the vertical channel and the horizontal channel, for the Glory of God and the good of multitudes!

Let me close by echoing the "Archimedes formula", and applying it to prayer. "If I could find a fulcrum that is strong enough, and a lever that is long enough, and a position or place to stand that is apart from that which I am trying to move, *I could move the world.*" Let me conclude with an explanation of the formula. For a Christian, and with regard to prayer, the "fulcrum" is the *purpose of God* (so it is plenty strong enough). An example of His purpose? Psalm 2:8 is one: "Ask of Me, and I will give you the heathen for your inheritance, and the uttermost parts of the earth for your possession." If a Christian doesn't have the answer, he is not asking! The "lever" is prayer, whose reach is limitless (so it is plenty long enough). The "position or place to stand" is "in Christ" (!!!!!). Pull over and park a moment, engines running, at this last sentence. You see, we Christians do not stand in the world witnessing for Christ; we stand in Christ witnessing to the world! I am in Christ, and nothing can reach me without His permission, and His permission is only given for HIS PURPOSES! This position "in Christ" is "apart from the world", and as long as I maintain the position and utilize its (HIS) authority and power, I CAN MOVE THE WORLD FOR HIS SAKE, and this means that multitudes of people will get swept into His movement! Remember that the lever is prayer.

Chapter 9

THE MASTER'S PRAYER

(Read John 17:1-26)

This is the "Holy of Holies" of revealed truth. Here, we eavesdrop at the eternal throne, and we must be reverent, studiously diligent and cautious.

Commentator J. C. Macaulay said, "This chapter is generally spoken of as a prayer: and in a manner that is true, yet there is something so lofty, so entirely beyond what constitutes prayer for us, that I prefer to designate it *communion*. The words 'I pray' indeed occur three times in our English version, but even there the Greek word so translated is one never used of man praying to God. It is the verb which signifies *making request on the plane of an equal*. So in this prayer, as it is called, our Lord does not *petition* the Father, but stands on the ground of divine equality presenting august desires which meet with immediate response in that relation of perfect oneness within the Godhead." G. Campbell Morgan supports Macaulay's assessment with this comment, "The word for prayer used here often occurs in the New Testament, but it is never used of *prayer* except by John, and he never uses it of any prayers other than the prayers of Jesus." In <u>An Expository Dictionary of New Testament Words</u>, W. E. Vines says that this word means "the petitioner is on a footing of equality or familiarity with the person whom he requests. It is used of a king in making request from another king, as in Luke 14:32. It describes asking upon equal terms."

Furthermore, this prayer was clearly not prayed in a private place or in a merely mental way. In verse 13, Jesus said, "These things I am speaking in the world," that is, *in their hearing before My Last Steps are taken on earth.* Unlike most of the prayers of Jesus, this prayer was *intended to be overheard and recorded-- for our instruction.*

The Gospel of John is "the mountain range of Scripture," and John 17 is the "Mount Everest." Picture this in a diagram in your mind. See the erratic skyline or horizon of a range of mountains before you. Then see one majestically high mountain rising far above the others. That one mountain corresponds to John 17.

You may recall the scene in John Bunyan's allegorical Christian classic, <u>Pilgrim's Progress,</u> in which Pilgrim, or Christian, is taken up on a high mountain to be given a view of his larger surroundings. He has abandoned the City of Destruction and is bound for the City of Light (about which he knows little). From the mountain, he is able to see the path that is behind him, and more importantly to him, he is able to see the spires of the golden city which is before him. He is renewed by the view and commits himself again to the rigors of the journey. Bunyan calls this mountain *"Mount Perspective." John 17 is the Mount Perspective of Jesus, of the Bible, of the church, of each individual follower of Christ.* From the lofty peak of this chapter, Jesus looks back into the infinity of eternity (from our limited perspective, we speak of it as *past*, or *"eternity past"*). He speaks of "the glory I had with Thee before the world was." "With Thee" is *para soi*. *Para* is used consistently throughout John's Gospel to picture an intimate spiritual association. Here, Jesus looks back and remembers "the glory He had with the Father" before the world was. Later in John 17, He will look *forward* into "eternity future" and anticipate a return to that glory Himself, and there He reveals *the Divine purpose to include us in that future glory* (vs 24)! From the peak of Mount Perspective, Jesus clearly views the "eternal past," the present "hour" (vs 1), and the "eternal future". When we follow His gaze and capture His understanding of these perspectives, we begin to understand how gigantic and majestic this chapter really is.

This prayer was clearly not prayed in a private place or in a merely mental way. It was offered in the hearing of His disciples and for their instruction. It was intended to be overheard and recorded to form a manual for our learning.

I. Parallels Between the Model Prayer and the Master's Prayer

Look first at some parallels between the Model prayer of Matthew 6 and the Master's prayer of John 17. Each is addressed to the "Father" (6 times in the Master's prayer). Heaven was as near to the soul of Jesus as the name "Father." It is not a God afar off Whom Jesus is addressing, but One with Whom the Son is walking in immediate, intimate communion, in perfect oneness of understanding, purpose and will. The phrase, "which art in heaven" in the Model prayer, is expressed by the epithets "holy" (vs 11) and "righteous" (vs 25) in the Master's prayer.

The phrase, "Hallowed be Thy Name" in the Model prayer is echoed in the Master's prayer by four references to God's "name." In both prayers, God's will is paramount. In both prayers, prayer asks for deliverance and protection from evil. In both prayers, prayer is never merely individual, but is corporate and intercessory. In the Model prayer, the pronouns that refer to believers are all plural – "our, us, we." The one praying is simply not permitted by the Model prayer to be individualistic and selfish. Similarly, in the Master's prayer, constant references are made to "they" and "them," identified as "the men You gave Me." *Jesus lived an "inside-out" life, focused on others, and He carefully instructs His followers to do the same.* This corporate emphasis is reinforced in the Master's prayer by a strong appeal for unity among His followers.

II. The Purpose of the Master's Prayer

Secondly, we see the *purpose* of the Master's prayer. In verse two, Jesus expressed both the immediate purpose and the ultimate purpose of the entire economy of God. "Glorify Thy Son, that the Son may glorify Thee." The word "glory" (or some variant of it) occurs 3 times in the first five verses, and each refers to a different time-frame. Here are the three occurrences in their three time-frames.

1. *The Present reference*

In verse 1, Jesus said, "Father, the *hour is come*; *glorify Thy Son*, that the Son may glorify Thee." This is a **present** reference, pointing to the redeeming event of the Cross/Resurrection. "The hour has come," Jesus announced. This is the hour which had been appointed before the world came into being. The entire purpose of God centered in this hour, and all history had been converging upon it. "The hour" was a byword between the Father and the Son, and the Son had tried to add it to the primary vocabulary of His few innermost friends. It was the hour of the fiery baptism of the Cross. "The hour" would be filled with pain, darkness, anguish, humiliation and death. In the face of that hour, what is the request of the equal but obedient Son of the Father? "*Deliver* Thy Son?" No! "*Sustain* Thy Son?" No! Rather, "*Glorify* Thy Son!" The glory He seeks here is an acquired glory, an attained glory, granted by the Father to the Incarnate Son as the Father's response to the Son's perfect work on earth. Jesus the Son would glorify the Father in the highest way on the Cross, and here, Jesus appeals to the *Father* that *He* may "glorify Thy Son, *that the Son may glorify Thee.*"

In presenting this petition to His Father, Jesus is asking for, and accepting, all that is involved in His glorification. He knows that His way to glorification is the way of the Cross. When He prays this prayer, He prays it with glad acceptance of all that is involved (see Hebrews 2:2).

2. *The Past reference*

The second use of the word "glory" is seen in verse 4, where Jesus said, "I have finished the work Thou gavest Me to do; I have glorified Thee on the earth." This is a reference to the immediate **past** -- a reference to His earthly incarnation and His training of the Twelve. The tenses of the verbs indicate completed action, and only an imposed interpretation can force them to mean something anticipated. In His incarnation, Jesus revealed the Father (and would also redeem men, but this is still future at this moment). In His training of the Twelve, He guaranteed future generation reproduction. It is my firm conviction that Jesus is referring here to two accomplished purposes: His revelation of the Father during the days of His incarnation, and His reproduction of His purpose and strategy in the training of His eleven "apostolic disciples." Again, it is His revelation of the Father, and His training of His immediate disciples for spiritual reproduction and multiplication throughout the remainder of human history that He refers to here. The other purpose of His incarnation, the purpose to redeem sinners by His Death on the Cross and His resurrection, will be highlighted just a short time later. Meantime, His Personal revelation of the Father and His purposeful training of His men for world impact through making disciples—these things have been accomplished.

There have been entire libraries of books written about the amazing life of Christ, and they are filled with commentary and interpretation on the amazing things Jesus did—the multitudes who followed Him, the miracles He performed, and the things He said. But Jesus indicates in this prayer in John 17 that all of that was done with the intention of reaching, teaching and training eleven men. And having done that, He says in verse 4, "I have accomplished the work Thou gavest Me to do." So this was one of the most important things He came to do—to train eleven men to the point of spiritual reproduction and multi-generational multiplication. He wasn't overly concerned about the multitudes who left Him and went back. His strategy centered in these eleven Galilean peasants (Judas, the traitor, was the only one from Judea). These eleven men were all He had to show for His ministry. But His strategy has worked! Furthermore, the vain attempts of the church to major on (often only imploding, self-serving) institutions, crowds, and other subtle substitutes which replace His original plan of "turning people into disciples," have predictably failed. What else can account for the staggering fact that two-fifths of the human race has not had satisfactory exposure to His Gospel of redemption? Our self-gratifying implosion of churches (and happily, there are some exceptions) is a far cry from the explosion which resulted in the Book of Acts from Jesus' strategy of training eleven men for the purpose of total world impact. Do not misrepresent these words. The local church is the very center of Christ's purposes on earth, but the local church is not merely a place of worship, fellowship, stewardship, and discipleship. It is also to be the base for a movement that penetrates to every language, tribe, people, nation, **and individual** on earth. And the strategy Jesus modeled and mandated is simplified in one command: "Turn people into disciples" (Matthew 28:19). Jesus has always worked through the principle of incarnation—God's life planted in individual people and moving out into others through them. Here is the "secret" systematized, the strategy summarized:

God living in a transparent human being, as in Jesus.

God longing to get into others through such a person, as He did in Jesus.

God in Christ's disciples lingering with other individuals to turn them into disciples who will be catalysts for world impact through multi-generational multiplication (as Jesus Himself did).

3. *The Prospective reference*

In verse 5, Jesus said, "Father, glorify Thou Me in Thy presence with the glory which I had with Thee before the world was made." This is the third occurrence of the word "glory" in Jesus' prayer for Himself. This is a ***prospective*** reference, expressing a request based on the relationship of Father and Son in eternity past. This prayer would begin to be answered at His Ascension. Furthermore, He indicates later that it is His purpose to include each of His followers (!) in His eternal glory (vs 24).

When the provinces of Alsace and Lorraine were returned to France after the war of 1914-1918, the restoration was on the ground of previous right, because that territory had been taken from France by Germany in 1871. Even so, Jesus here asks for glory which was His by previous right. However, His original glory had not been taken from him, as the French territories were taken from France by Germany. No, Jesus voluntarily gave up the glory He shared with the Father in heaven before the world was, coming to the earth as a man in order to redeem us sinners (see Philippians 2:5-8). Still, He was asking that He be restored to His original glory with the Father.

What amazing revelations about Jesus (and about God) are contained in His request to be glorified. His pre-existence, *eternal* pre-existence, is indicated here. Furthermore, He had a place of co-existence, co-equality, co-eternality, a place of honor by the Father's side in that eternal pre-existence. Also, there was a glory of being, *shared without division in the equal and eternal Godhead.* What a commentary there is in the Master's prayer about the Trinity, the Trinality, the tri-unitarian nature of God. The inter-relations shared between the Father and the Son should be carefully studied in the Master's prayer. Now Jesus is asking that the very glory He had with the Father should crown and encompass His humanity, for He prays as the Son of Man. Did you know that humanity (like yours, but without sin) has been glorified with the very glory of God, in the Person of our blessed and all-glorious Lord, Jesus Christ?

III. The Partitions of the Master's Prayer

Thirdly, we will note *the partitions*, or divisions, of the Master's prayer.

The Master's Prayer

1. *The Individual feature*

In the first division of the prayer, we see the *individual feature* of His prayer. In verses 1-5, Jesus prays for Himself. First, before He turns to the other concerns which dominate His heart, the Son prays for Himself. Again, we must exercise care and caution, because even His prayer for Himself is presented in special relation to the power over all men which the Father has given to Him (vs 2a), and in relation to His own grace to the sons of men (2b).

At each of the divisions of the Master's prayer, the believer can find an example for his own praying. Here is a clear warrant for praying for yourself, and it is re-inforced often in the remainder of the New Testament. A good example is found in the great request of Paul in Romans 15:30-32, where the Apostle seeks to enlist the Roman Christians to pray for him. In his entreaty, he says, "I beseech you, brethren, ... that ye strive together *with me* in your prayers to God for me." No Christian should ask others to pray for him if he does not pray for himself!

2. *The Intercessory factor*

In the second division of the prayer, we see the *intercessory factor* of His prayer. In the longest section of the prayer, verses 6I-19, Jesus prays for His apostolic group of disciples. Commentator H. R. Reynolds says, "For Himself He has little to ask, but as soon as His word takes the form of intercession for His own, it becomes an irresistible stream of the most fervent love. Sentence rushes upon sentence with wonderful power, yet the repose is never disturbed." The Master's prayer recorded in John 17 may be viewed as the model and pattern of His intercession in heaven throughout this church age.

Again, the Christian should take both the kind and substance of the Master's prayer as his personal example. In kind, the Master's prayer is intercessory in nature. A great portion of the believer's prayers should be intercessory, and the blessings sought for others should be spiritual in nature, like the requests of Jesus for His disciples in this prayer. In substance, Jesus gave us a vast field of spiritual concerns to pray for. The section below on "the petitions of the Master's prayer" will provide a full gamut of concerns for the personal "prayer list" of all disciples today.

3. *The Indefinite future*

In the final division of the prayer, we see the Christian movement, the disciple-making Plan, extended into the **indefinite future**. This section is apparently sub-divided into two parts, and both concern the future. Verses 20-23 concern the indefinite future, the remainder of human history. In these verses, Jesus prays for all future followers throughout the remainder of history. Verses 24-26 include the infinite future (eternity). In fact, it seems that the last three verses summarize the entire movement from eternity to eternity. Here are the summary points: The Father "sent" the Son (vs 25b), presupposing the pre-existence of the Son with the Father for all eternity "past", and presupposing the glory They shared "before the world was." This also highlights the Incarnation of Christ as the "Sent One" in human flesh. During the earthly Incarnation, He "declared unto them the Father's Name" (vs 26a), and the movement will continue after His departure by the same strategy – "and I will declare it" (vs 26b). So throughout Christian history, Jesus (through the Presence and power of His Other Self, the Holy Spirit), will "manifest the Father's Name unto those the Father gives Him", as in verse 6. Then, when history has ended, His

The Master's Prayer

followers will be with Him where He is, and will behold the glory which the Father will give to the Son – and this destiny will be *eis tous aionos ton aionon*, "into the ages of the ages" (vs 24)!!!!! The infinite future is graciously guaranteed for the child of God!

Years ago, a great German Christian named Eric Sauer wrote a trilogy of books which present the entire Christian revelation. The first book was entitled <u>From Eternity to Eternity</u>, and attempted to give a panoramic view of the entire revelation of God. In the Master's prayer, He draws concentric circles, with Himself in the central circle, then moving into and through the second circle, His immediate twelve "apostolic disciples," then outward and forward through history to the end, and *the entire picture is framed between two "eternities."* And as born-agains, you and I are included all the way *from eternity to eternity.*

Again, the Master's prayer sets the example for our praying. Every Christian should be so locked into the strategy of Jesus to "turn people into disciples" that his interests, his plans, his actions, *and his anticipations of the future* should focus on the generations of disciples God will give through his training of the present generation of disciples God gives to him *(just like Jesus).* Jesus saw the masses through the man, and built the man to impact the masses – not only in the present, but clearly in the future as well. In this prayer, Jesus sees rising before His eyes the multitudes in all ages who would believe their testimony as if those future believers were already believing! And every disciple should be able to do the same. He should be so confident of the strategy of Jesus and of His total obedience to that strategy that he should know that future generations of his own disciples are as certain as they were for Jesus. Do not misunderstand the previous sentence. Every Christian is to be a disciple of

Christ, but the responsibility for his emergence is assigned to a disciple-maker, and if someone does not assume the specific responsibility to build him into a disciple, the process will be aborted again, as is often the case, by default.

IV. The Petitions of the Master's Prayer

His petitions (that is, His requests) focus historically upon His disciples, both present (vss 6-19) and future (vss 20-26). He establishes their *Identity* by two descriptions (vss 6-8): (1) His disciples are those who have *openly and fully adhered to His name and have been fully joined to His Person (vs 6a)*; (2) His disciples are those who have *openly and fully accepted His words and adjusted to them (vs 6c)*. Having established their identity, He then makes six petitions concerning them:

1. For the Unity of His followers

He prays for the **unity** of His followers, vss 11, 21. At this point, there are four closely allied concepts which must be clearly distinguished. One is *unanimity* (of opinion). This is not mandatory in the fellowship of believers, though deliberate disagreement for the sake of asserting self is intolerable. A second concept is *uniformity* (of organization or ritual). This is not mandatory in the fellowship of believers. A third concept is *union* (of affiliation). This is not mandatory in the fellowship of believers. The fourth concept is *unity* (oneness of inner heart and essential purpose). This, I believe, is what Jesus prays for in this prayer.

The unity of Jesus' followers comes from the association each one has with the Father's name. In the Bible, names are very significant, because the name a person bears is representative of his nature and character. The Psalmist said, "Some boast in chariots, and some in horses; but we will boast in the name of the Lord our God" (Psalm 20:7). Jesus sought to build unity among His disciples by showing both in His life and His teaching the personality and character of the Father; that is, He revealed His "name." The more a disciple understands the attributes and character of God, the more he will experience unity with other disciples of the same mind.

One of the most incisive Christian writers in the English-speaking world was A. W. Tozer. Tozer illustrated Christian unity with these words: "Has it ever occurred to you that one hundred pianos all tuned to the same tuning fork are automatically tuned to each other? They are of one accord by being tuned, not to each other, but to another standard to which each one must individually bow. So when one hundred worshippers meet together, each one looking away to Christ, they are in heart nearer to each other than they could possibly be were they to become 'unity conscious' and turn their eyes away from Christ to strive for closer fellowship with each other." Dear Christian, ponder these words carefully, and then prove them in every contact with other Christians. When each Christian maintains a heart and a gaze fixed upon Christ, there will be the unity among believers which Jesus prayed for.

2. *For the Serenity of His followers*

He prays for the *serenity* of His followers. In verse 13, Jesus said, "But now I come to Thee; and these things I speak in the world, that they may have My joy made full in themselves." Throughout His prayer, Jesus admits that His followers will face much adversity through history. Here, He reveals how important it is that His people find and maintain "the peace of God, which passes understanding." He speaks of His joy filling His people.

Christians seldom realize the Biblical perspective of joy. Sam Shoemaker often said, "The infallible sign of the Presence of God is not faith, or love, but joy." Another said, "Joy is the flag that flies over the King's castle when King Jesus is in residence."

Jesus is here praying for the joy which has its origin in heaven. As C. S. Lewis said, "Joy is the serious business of heaven." One pastor said, "Joy is waking up in the middle of the night, remembering that you belong to God, and turning over and going back to sleep happy because of it." Heaven's joy is not dependent on earthly circumstances, and Christians must be filled with the joy of Christ.

Sudden thought: Can you imagine a choir, made up of demons, directed by the devil, singing about the glories of wickedness, or the happiness of hell? No, indeed! It's the message of forgiveness, hope, and eternal life that sets the soul to singing. I like the way one brother closed a letter: "Until further notice, celebrate everything!" If we do, we can help to answer the Master's prayer.

3. *For the Security of His followers*

He prays for the **security** of His followers in verses 11-12 and 15-16. In these two brief sections of the prayer, Jesus prays for two kinds of security for His people.

In verse 12, He prays about their *perfect preservation* in *eternal security*. "While I was with them in the world, I kept them in Thy name: those that Thou gavest me I have kept, and none of them is lost, but the son of perdition; that the Scripture might be fulfilled."

A man walking in a New England cemetery saw this epitaph on a gravestone: "Kept!" This is the idea of our eternal security in Christ. We are kept. Helmut Thielicke, the great German preacher, said, "He who is safe in eternity does

The Master's Prayer

not need to fear what time can bring." A Christian is not just saved, he is *safe*.

Then He prays for their *providential protection* in *everyday situations*. He requests that "You should keep them from the evil."

Jesus prayed, "Holy Father, keep through Thine own name those whom Thou has given me." Someone told of a ship that went down years ago off the coast of California. There were not enough life boats on board to accommodate all the passengers, and many were left to perish. But there was a mother who saw to it that her son, a boy of eight years of age, had a place among the rescued, though she herself had to be left behind. As he tearfully boarded the boat, she pushed into his hand a note which she had hastily written. It was addressed to the boy's father, who would be waiting for him in San Francisco. In part, the note said, "My darling, since I, his mother, loved him well enough to die for him, you, his father, must keep him with the tenderest care." Jesus is saying something like that. "My Father, since I, your Son, loved them well enough to die for them, You, Father, must keep them in Your tenderest care." And He does!

4. *For the Sanctity of His followers*

He prays for the **sanctity** (or **sanctification**) of His followers, verses 17-19. You see, the disciples of Jesus needed *perfecting (maturing)* as well as *preserving*. And this is always true of His followers.

In verse 17, Jesus prayed, "Sanctify them through Thy truth: Thy word is truth." Then, in verse 19, He said, "For their sakes I sanctify Myself, that they might be sanctified through Thy truth." The term "sanctification" requires very careful, technical, spiritual attention. It is used in two primary ways in the Bible. There are essentially two kinds of sanctification taught in the Word of God. One is *positional* and *perfect*; this is the "setting apart" of *sinful human beings* by God the Father, God the Son, and God the Holy Spirit for *eternal salvation*. The other is *practical* and *progressive*. It is the "setting apart" *progressively* of *saved people* for *purity of life* and *practically* for the *service of God*. In Jesus' prayer in John 17:17-19, Jesus prays for the sanctification of His followers, and He declares His own sanctification. What does this mean? We must be careful to see clearly the *meaning* of sanctification in these verses. When Jesus said to the Father, "Sanctify them," He was praying for their progressive purity and their practical usefulness in this world. "Father, set them apart" for these things. When He said, "For their sakes I sanctify Myself," He meant that He had devoted, consecrated, "set Himself apart" for the accomplishment of His assignment. Note that even this full devotion of Himself to the Father was *for the sake of His followers*.

Just a note of interpretation. The word "sanctification" is often interpreted as if it meant progressive purification only (and it is even used by some Christian groups to speak of sinless perfection). But the Biblical word "sanctify" is not used so much for deliverance from the defilement of sin as for separation from common use to sacred use. Biblically, objects and places are often referred to as "holy" or "sanctified," and it surely cannot be supposed that they were delivered from the corruption of sinfulness. No, this means that they were employed for God's special and sacred purposes. Also, it should be carefully noted that Jesus said in this prayer, "I sanctify Myself." This is not a progressive deliverance from sinfulness, but rather a separation from any other purpose in order to do the Father's will and complete the assignment He had been given by His Father. This is the primary meaning of sanctification in the Bible. However, let me be quick to add

The Master's Prayer

that, if a believer is truly set apart unto God and His purpose, *he will be progressively delivered from any residual sin that remains in his life.* For us, this sanctification is a lifelong process.

But we not only see the meaning of sanctification here, we can also see the *means* by which it occurs. The sanctification (or full consecration) of Jesus to His assigned task took place by means of His *will*, but our sanctification to progressive purity and practical usefulness takes place "through Thy truth", and "Thy word is truth" (vs 17). The sanctification (or devotion) of Jesus to His task was "in order that they (His followers) might be sanctified *through the truth*" (vs 19). So our progressive purity and practical usefulness will only occur as we have regular and rich exposure to the truth of the Word of God. Only as we live in and by the truth of the Bible will we be pure and productive.

In John 15:3, Jesus said, "Now ye are clean through the words which I have spoken unto you." In Ephesians 5:25, we are "cleansed through the washing of water by Word"; that is, the Word of God does a laundering work on our inner lives and conditions our outer conduct so that we can be powerful and productive for Him.

5. *About the Duty of His followers*

Then Jesus prayerfully specifies the ***duty*** of His followers, vss 17, 21-23. "As Thou hast sent Me into the world, even so have I also sent them into the world . . . . that the world may know that Thou hast sent Me, and hast loved them, as Thou hast loved Me . . . that the world may believe." His strategy of protection for His disciples is seen by coupling verses 14 and 16, "I have given them Thy word; and the world hath hated them, because they are not of the world, even as I am not of the world; .... They are not of the world, even as I am not of the world." Now, focus on the verse between those verses: "I pray not that Thou shouldest take them out of the world, but that Thou shouldest keep them from the evil."

So Jesus' strategy for world impact begins with the truth that His disciples are to be *in* the world, but not "*of*" the world. This means several things vocationally for a Christian.

One, it means that he is not to be *isolated* from the world. It is a serious, even tragic, misreading of Jesus to think that "separation from the world" means removal from the people and life of the world. This removal, or isolation, was the stance of the Pharisees (their very name means, "separated ones"). A Christian's protection is in his *insulation in Christ*, not in his *isolation from his community and its culture*. Both the negative aspect, our protection, and the positive aspect, our vocation, must be re-examined with great care by the disciples of Jesus today. Why? Because the tendency of Christians is to isolate themselves in local churches, the "Christian ghetto," and remain untouched and undisturbed by the world's need. In turn, they seldom touch the world with life and wholeness, and the world rots on toward its final destruction. The church building itself allows Christians to be monastic and escapist. It becomes our escape device, our ejection hatch, our hideaway from the world. When this occurs, the believer becomes what John Stott called "a rabbit-hole Christian," able only to see the tunnel inside and the tiny bit of light which is allowed from outside.

Second, the prayer of Jesus that the Christian be "in the world, but not of it" means that he is not to allow the *assimilation* of himself into the values and attitudes of his world. "Be not conformed to this world," the Bible clearly says (Romans 12:2). Conformity to the world will, in time, mean the loss of Christian identity for the believer. There will finally be no distinguishable difference between him and the world. The

Christian must not allow this absorption of himself into the Godless world system.

Third, the prayer of Jesus means that the Christian is to engage in purposeful *mission* in the world by *investing his life, his testimony, his influence, his prayers – all that he is and has – into the world-impacting strategy of Jesus.* He is to be in the world, involved in presenting Christ while keeping himself insulated from the evil of the world. As salt, he must get out of the "salt shaker" (the church) and into the "salad" and "potatoes" (places of practical ministry in his society). As light, he must penetrate the deep darkness of this ignorant and sinful world. Every person he meets will be seen as a potential brother or sister in Christ, and he will act to bring that person to Him. Once he is won to Christ, the disciple who brought him to Christ will become his discipler, now involving him in the strategy of Jesus.

6. *About the Destiny of His followers*

Jesus also prayerfully specifies the ***destiny*** of His followers, vss 24-25. He says two things about their destiny with Him: (1) His followers will *be with Him—eternally (!)*, 24, and (2) His followers will *behold His glory—eternally (!)*, 25

A little boy and his father went into a pet store to buy a dog for the boy. All the dogs looked as though they would have made good pets, but one in particular put on a "happy show" for the man and the boy, wagging his tail so wildly that it looked like his entire body was controlled by the wagging tail. When the time to choose came, the boy didn't hesitate. He said, "Dad, I want the one with the 'happy ending'." Friends, all of God's born-agains, all of His children, are headed for a happy ending! We will get to be with Jesus, and behold His glory – forever! His Book indicates that

The Daily Quiet Time

He will never get tired of being kind to us (Ephesians 2:7), and we surely will never get tired of Him!

V. The Process of Disciple-making Revealed in the Master's Prayer

The process of disciple-making revealed in the Master's prayer will be reproduced in the life of every faithful disciple-Maker! Here are the steps that are detectable in Jesus' training of the Twelve.

God gave His disciples to Jesus— vss 6, 9, 10b, 11, 12. *So you must depend on God to get a disciple.* One of my primary "Timothys" is a great disciple/disciple-maker named Dan Baugh, who lives in Lake Jackson, Texas. I have heard Dan make this statement several times: "All the disciples I have enlisted have not produced in the disciple-making process, but *the disciples whom God sent to me have never failed."* This has been totally true in my experience as well. Personally, I have never solicited or enlisted a single disciple, and I have *(by the grace of God)* a considerable number of disciples.

They responded in faith to His Person & faithfully to the training process— vss 6, 8, 26. *The disciple God gives to you will follow Jesus and will be faithful in training; then, He will multiply disciples through him to the ends of the earth and until the end of time.* This statement presupposes that you will thoroughly master and follow the strategy of Jesus in building disciples. This will mean that a concept of at least four-generational multiplication (see II Timothy 2:2) will be built into your personal disciple in such a manner that he will transfer the same concept to his disciple, ...

Jesus gave them the Father's word, vss 6a, 8, 13a, 14, 26. You will not make disciples unless you consistently teach them (close up and personal) the sure and solid and systematic truths of the Word of God in purposeful settings.

It is only through the Word of God that men believe in Christ unto salvation. Romans 10:17 lays down the definitive rule: "Faith comes by hearing, and hearing by the Word of God." In the Divine economy, this rule is observed without exception. In the Master's prayer, He draws the future into the present and prays for "them also who shall believe on Me through their word." "Their" refers to the "apostolic disciples", the Apostles, who were with Jesus when He prayed this prayer. The old commentator, John Brown, said of the Apostolic contribution, "Before they died, the apostles of Christ, under the guidance of the Holy Spirit, embodied in the books of the New Testament their doctrine and its evidence, gave an account of what they had taught, and of the miraculous works which had proved that they were taught of God. In these writings, they still continue to testify of the Son. The apostles alone are 'God's ambassadors' in the strict sense. They alone stand 'in Christ's stead' (II Cor. 5:20). They had 'the mind of Christ' in a sense peculiar to themselves, and that mind is in their writings." It is the truth embodied is these New Testament books which we as Christian disciples are to proclaim to men.

Furthermore, not only are sinners saved by hearing the Word of God, but saints are also cleansed, consecrated, matured and sanctified (separated unto God for His use) by hearing and obeying the Word of God. Jesus said of the "apostolic disciples," "They have kept Thy word" (John 17:6). He said, "I have given them Thy word" (vs 14). Then He prayed for future disciples, "Sanctify them through Thy truth: Thy word is truth" (vs 17), and further, "And for their sakes I sanctify Myself, that they also might be sanctified through the truth" (vs. 19). Note in each statement the instrumentality of the Word of God. Jesus calls it "the truth," and what God says in His Word is truth *per se*. Dear Christian, you are totally responsible to "turn people into disciples" (Matthew 28:19—the Great Commission!), and this cannot be done without the *sure, solid, and systematic teaching of the Word of God to the potential disciple.* If you are obeying the command of Jesus and building disciples, you are systematically teaching them the rich truths of the Word of God.

Jesus staked His entire ministry on these men, vss 9-10. Jesus prayed for them as the precious fruit of His life-labor. The Living Bible says in vs 10, "And all of them, since they are mine, belong to You; and You have given them back to Me with everything else of Yours, and so *they are My glory!" Your disciples will be your joy and your crown (I Thess. 2:19-20; Philippians 4:1).* Observe Jesus carefully at this point. He said, "For their sakes I sanctify Myself, that they also might be sanctified through the truth" (vs 18). **It is as if His own ministry were merely subordinate to theirs**! This is the spirit of every true disciple-maker. He sublimates his own desires to the needs of his disciples. He probates His own success upon their productivity.

Jesus sent them (remember, they are also called "Apostles," the "sent ones") into the world for a specific *purpose* and with adequate *provisions*—vss 18, 20 (note that the focus is on "future believers"), 21b, 23b. *You will watch in gratitude and amazement as your disciples go global—for total world impact!* If your disciple is not seeking enlarging impact to the ends of the earth, he is not properly built! And if he has true world vision (as every disciple should), and a strategy to fulfill it (as every disciple should), he *will have impact to the ends of the earth.*

Jesus promised that they would live in His Presence forever, and that He would share with them His own ultimate and eternal glory—24. Disciple-making means that you may be used of God to increase the number of those in heaven to "a multitude which no man can number"!

VI. The Passionate Priority of the Master's Prayer

Jesus said to His Father, "Thou hast given Him (Thy Son) power over all flesh, that He should give eternal life to as many as Thou hast given Him; And this is life eternal, that they might know Thee the only true God, and Jesus Christ, whom Thou hast sent" (vss 2, 3).

The passionate priority of God is to give eternal life to human beings. What is it to have eternal life? What was John Bunyan's Pilgrim seeking when he put his fingers in his ears and ran from the City of Destruction, crying, "Life! Life! Eternal life!" He was not seeking eternal existence, but eternal *right* existence. This eternal life, according to Jesus, is a matter of "knowing God, and Jesus Christ, whom He has sent." Note several key things.

Note, first, that the names of God and of Jesus are put on a level as objects of faith. This is incompatible with the view that Jesus is a mere man. *Eternal life could never be made to depend on knowing any mere man.* And yet, it depends on knowing Jesus. So Jesus is not a mere man! Jesus is God!

Another key idea is that knowing Jesus is having eternal life. This "knowing" Christ refers to is an intimate relationship with Him. The Old Testament regularly uses the word "know" for sexual relations, as in "Adam knew Eve his wife; and she conceived, and bare Cain" (Gen 4:1). So the idea of knowing suggests a mutual experience and exchange. Thus, we can deduce this definition: eternal life is relationship with God in which there is a mutual exchange of life between Him and the believer, and requires continuing intimate interaction between God and the believing human being.

In the New Testament, eternal life is clearly more than, and profoundly different from, the idea of mere unending existence. Life is more than prolonged being, and eternity is more than mere endlessness. In fact, both "eternity" and "eternal life" would be better understood if we say that those words involve *the negation of time altogether.* Both eternity and eternal life involve "the eternal *now,*" because however long either may last, it is still only, always *now.* For example, a life that lasted 32 billion years would still only be lived as *now.* Though eternal life is a *permanent* (!) possession, it is also a *present* possession. Jesus said, "He who hears my word (present tense), and believes (present tense) on Him who sent Me, has (present tense!) eternal life, and shall (future tense) never ('never' means *never ever)* perish, but is passed (perfect tense) from death into life" (John 5:24). One commentator called eternal life "the condition of *aionian* blessedness." The word *aionian* describes both length ('everlasting') and quality (life that is full of God).

In *duration,* eternity is *the lifetime of God.* Since you were born, He has included you in its length. However, that is not enough. He would love to also include you in its *quality* ('eternal life'). Eternal life is that life that has Jesus Christ at its very center now, and will be lived out with Him in Heaven forever.

This is the priority of Jesus in His prayer. Have you faced up to His desire to give you the gift of eternal life? Think of it. *In one moment of time,* you can receive the gift of *eternal life!* That one moment of time hurries by, but eternal life lasts forever. How do you receive eternal life?

The good news of eternal life can only be real to you if you first confess some bad news about yourself. You are a sinner, and if you remain in your sins, you are disqualified from eternal life. In order to escape your sins and their judgment, you must confess those sins directly to the One against whom you have sinned. "Lord, I have sinned, and my sins deserve hell. I am sorry for my sins, and want to have freedom from them. You have said that You love me in spite of my sins, and that Jesus died for me because of your love. You have also said that He rose again from the dead after paying for my sins, and that if I would trust Him, Him alone, to save me, He would come into my life in the moment of my faith in Him, would forgive my sins, and give me the gift of eternal life. Jesus, I do now trust You and You alone to save me. Come into my life and take over. I receive You and trust You, and I thank You for fulfilling Your Word. Take my life at this moment and use me for Your glory. In Your Name I pray. Amen."

Now look back over the Master's prayer in John 17 and consider some ways you can cooperate with the Holy Spirit in seeing Jesus' desires fulfilled in your life and your world today.

Chapter 10

PRAYER THAT PREVAILS

John 15:7: *"If ye abide in Me, and my words abide in you, ye shall ask what ye will, and it shall be done unto you."*

Can there be any question that Jesus Christ expected — and received — answers to His prayers? None whatsoever. And in all of His recorded teachings, He leads us to believe that we (also) shall be able to obtain, through prayer, what otherwise would not be ours.

However, we have only to compare the promises of Jesus and the experience of Christians as seen consistently in their biographies or personal confessions, to discover a wide difference between *His assurances* with regard to prayer and *their actual experiences* in prayer. These variations are often so wide that Christians lower their expectations concerning answers to prayer, and finally pray only in a mediocre manner, governed more by unbelief than by faith.

In a recent "Peanuts" cartoon, Lucy said to Linus, "If you hold your hands upside down, you get the opposite of what you pray for." Many Christians must feel that they pray with their hands in the upside-down position! They have become so accustomed to disappointment in prayer that an unmistakable answer to prayer would shock them. All of us must confess a large measure of shame at this point. We have asked so many things which we have never received; we have sought so much without finding; we have knocked repeatedly, but the door has remained tightly closed. We have excused our failure by rationalizing that our prayer was probably not according to God's will, or that God withheld the answer to give something else, even something better. We forget that *if we prayed as we should, we would necessarily and inevitably ask what is according to His will*. If we "delight ourselves in the Lord, He will give us the desires of our hearts," because our desires are conditioned and determined by our delight in Him. He can trust that kind of prayer — and will favorably answer it. But we tend to evade the plain words of Christ, "Whatsoever ye shall ask in my name, that will I do."

We have only to selectively read the life stories of the great devotional saints (actually, *just Christians*) of history to see that they had discovered a great secret with regard to prayer and its answer, a secret which apparently has eluded many of us. A great library of prayers, intercessions, and supplications stands recorded in heaven, but some are answered, and some are not. What determines the difference? Why are some answered, and the prayers of some Christians answered *with regularity*, while the opposite is true of others?

We will turn for the answers to these questions to Christ's "legacy of love," the instructions He gave in His last lengthy interview, or "teaching session," with His disciples before the great redeeming events of His Death and Resurrection. These instructions are recorded in John thirteen through sixteen. In this crucial passage, Jesus gave the fullest instructions about prevailing prayer which He ever expressed.

We will focus on John fifteen, though we will range around that chapter in a wider circle, gathering *the prerequisites of prevailing prayer* which are stated by Jesus Himself. In this passage, Jesus teaches that any prayer which is to prevail with God and receive His favor and His answer, must pass five crucial (this word is based on the Latin word for "cross," and means "as serious as the cross") tests. It will be seen that these five tests could be regarded as only different shades of the same attitude. However, each is important for the testing of our prayers. Before we examine them, let me also add that these are not mere tests (a word which suggests only discipline and severity to some people); these are touchstones of delight to the surrendered and devoted heart.

I. SEEK THE GLORY OF GOD ALONE

First, if my prayers are to be favorably heard, and answered, I must be a person who *seeks the glory of God alone*. Jesus stated it as His own sole motive, "That the Father may be glorified in the Son" (John 14:13). The one and only purpose of Christ on earth was to glorify the Father, and at the close of His life here He was conscious that He had perfectly fulfilled this purpose. "Now is the Son of Man glorified, and God is glorified in Him." And this earthly satisfaction was perfectly consistent with, and an extension of, His eternal being. Each of the three Persons in the Holy Trinity has always been (and remains) devoted to upholding and displaying the moral beauty of the Other Two. The Father glorifies the Son and exalts the Spirit. The Son glorifies the Father and exalts the Spirit. And the Holy Spirit glories the Son and exalts the Father. This devotion for The Others is total and equal in Each Member of the Godhead at all times. Having completed His work of redemption and having sat down at the right hand of the Majesty on high, Christ still pursues His cherished purpose of making His Father known, loved, adored, and glorified. Thus, no prayer can hope to succeed with Him, with His Father, or with the Holy Spirit, which is out of harmony with this sublime and selfless intent.

Any prayer you offer to God should be consciously submitted to this standard — can I be confident in the Presence of Christ that my request will promote the glory of the Father? Marshall the evidence, present the reasons, and establish the grounds for your prayer. If your claim can be satisfactorily made "to the glory of God the Father," your prayer is already granted. But you may be sure that it is impossible to seek the glory of God consistently if selfish desires and aims dominate your life. Prayer is submitting to God and His glory, *not subverting God to yourself and your glory*. The glory of God and the glory of self can no more co-exist in the same person than light and darkness in the same space. The glory of God can only triumph in a man at the expense of self, and the glory of self can only triumph there at God's expense. Surely no one can truly *pray* for God's glory unless he is *living* for God's glory. The Christian who can state his motive in Paul's words, "That Christ may be glorified in my body, whether by life or by death," will touch the tenderest spot in Christ's glorified nature, and will awaken all of His mighty power in answer to his prayers. Christian, should we not (you and I) make a repentance-and-faith adjustment of our lives to the glory of God at this moment, so that God can show His promised answers to our prayers?

II. SUBMIT YOUR PRAYERS TO THE STANDARD OF CHRIST'S CHARACTER

Second, if my prayers are to be favorably heard, and answered, then I must *submit my prayers to the standard of Christ's character*. Jesus said, "Whatsoever ye shall ask *in My name*, that will I do." Throughout the Bible, a person's *name* stands for that person's *nature*. So Jesus said, You must ask *in My nature*. That is, when we pray, it must not be the self-nature that dictates the prayer, but the Christ-nature within the believer. But what are the distinguishing marks of the Christ-nature? The Christ-nature excludes boasting and practices humility. The Christ-nature is pure, peaceable, and loving. The Christ-nature is not swayed by the glare of the world. In short, the Christ-nature is full of Gethsemane, Calvary, Pentecost and Olivet. It is full of self-surrender, of the death-stance of the cross, of the breath of the Holy Spirit, and of the heavenly life of the Ascension.

Believer, get alone with God just now. Pour out your deepest heart to Him in prayer. Let the Christ-nature, which is in you by the Holy Spirit, speak to Christ Himself on the Throne of the universe. Thus, your heart becomes the prayer chapel for a dialogue between God the Father, God the Son, and God the Holy Spirit. This kind of prayer starts at the Throne of God as He governs your life, descends to you through a particular need (or *sense* of need), cycles through your heart as its prayer chapel, receives an answer, and then returns to God in the form of praise. Thus, the river of the water of life has descended from the Throne of God in the Eternal City, flowed right through your heart, and returned right back to its source. Its "outbound" course has sought the low point of your human need, and its "inbound" course has sought the high point of God's glory. It began with God's glory and ends with God's glory, and when it can find a matching point on earth, it will seek that point. It began with Christ's nature and it will end with Christ's nature, and when it can find a person who seeks consistency with His nature, it will hear and answer the prayer that is prayed according to the standard of that nature. This is what is meant by praying "in Christ's name."

If our prayers are to prevail with God and in behalf of men, we must get quiet enough before God to let the Christ-nature speak. We must be quiet and submissive enough that He can create our petitions at His throne and countersign them in our hearts, thus endorsing His own purposes by means of our answered prayers. If this litmus test were properly applied to our prayers, surely many of the petitions we now offer so idly would never leave our lips. We would rise far above our usual petty praying, and would occupy the heavenlies with Him, both in person and in purpose. Many a prayer of mine has been like a frail little boat, leaving the shore of my unschooled heart, only to be dashed to pieces on the steadfast rock of God's purpose. If I would only learn to pray according to the nature of Christ within me, that nature would *become* the rock to which my prayers would anchor. The name of Christ must be predominant in my conversation, and the nature of Christ must be predominant in my character, if I am to be effective in prayer. I must know the meaning of, and practice the discipline of, praying in submission to the standard of Christ's character.

III. STAY IN UNHINDERED UNION WITH HIM

Third, if my prayers are to be favorably heard, and answered, then I must *stay in unhindered union with Christ*. He said, "If ye abide in Me, ... ye shall ask what ye will, and it shall be done unto you" (John 15:7). The day you were saved, you were transplanted out of Adam as your representative man, and into Christ. You are now "in Christ," having been placed there by a miracle of the Holy Spirit at the moment of your trust in Jesus Christ. You entered into union with Christ at that moment, and that union is forever. However, its conscious enjoyment and practical usefulness will be real only as you "keep all channels open" between you and Christ. This is called "abiding in Christ."

You see, your arm may be in your body, and yet be dislocated and useless. If I were to board a train in Memphis, Tennessee, today, intending to go all the way to St. Louis, Missouri, all that would be necessary for me to arrive at my destination would be to resist the temptation to get off the train at any of the stations along the way. It would be necessary for me to remain on the train until I arrive at my chosen destination. That's the word — *remain*. Stay put. This is the meaning of the word, "abide." To abide in Christ is to *keep the contact intact* between me and Jesus. Like the rider on the train, the faithful Christian must be careful to resist every temptation or suggestion to depart from full communion with Him by any act (even the tiniest act) of disobedience or unbelief.

While you are abiding in Christ in daily fellowship and moment-by-moment communion, it will not be hard for you to pray accurately and confidently, because Jesus has promised to abide in you as you abide in Him. The very Life of Christ in the moving Presence of the Holy Spirit will work in you, producing in you desires and petitions similar to those which He ceaselessly presents to His Father. Throughout this age, Jesus has been asking of God the Father. This perpetual communion is the constant attitude of the Son toward the Father. He cannot ask what the Father will not give. So we may be sure of success when we get into the current of His prayer. Abide in Him so that He may freely abide in you, not only in the activities and routines of your daily life, but in the intercessions and supplications of the specific time of prayer as well. Your delight in Him will increase with communion, and your communion will increase with that delight. As the relationship remains unhindered, you may "ask what ye will, and it will be done unto you."

IV. SIFT YOUR PRAYERS THROUGH HIS WORDS

Fourth, if my prayers are to be favorably heard, and answered, I must *sift my prayers through the sieve of His words*. My life and prayers must be monitored by the Word of God. Jesus said, "If my words abide in you, ... ye shall ask what ye will, and it shall be done unto you" (John 15:7). Christ's words may be compared to a jury of wise and serious persons, sitting in the court of eternal reality to try my prayers before they pass on into the Father's presence. If His Word pronounces an unfavorable verdict on my prayers, they will not be answered. But if His Word gives approval to my prayers, they will be answered. Hearing His Word quickens me to ask on the basis of revelation. It was when Jesus *mentioned* the Living Water that the Samaritan woman said, "*Give* me *this* water." Her request was prompted and conditioned by His revelation.

Suppose that I pray a prayer that is earth-born and earth-bound, "of the earth, and earthy," and stained with selfishness. As the prayer approaches the throne of God, this verse stands like a sentinel at the throne: "Seek ye first the kingdom of God and His righteousness," and the prayer is turned away. I am surprised and ashamed by my own spiritual vagrancy, and I discard that prayer as unworthy of Christ's blessing.

Suppose I pray a prayer that is marred by criticism and unkindness towards another human being, even toward another Christian. That prayer is stopped in its tracks by this solemn word of Jesus: "Love your neighbor as yourself," or a broader word, "Love your enemies, and pray for them that despitefully use you," and the unworthy prayer hastens away from the holy Throne.

Or suppose I pray a prayer that is tainted by a heart of murmuring and complaint because of the weight of Christ's cross and the restraint of Christ's yoke. The sentinel of the Word touches me with the sword-point of this notable declaration of Jesus: "In the world ye shall have tribulation; but be of good cheer, for I have overcome the world," and I pull back, aware that the mixture of complaint with communion cannot be allowed in the Throne-chamber of heaven. Like the accusers of the woman taken in the act of adultery (John 8:1-11), prayers like these are inwardly convicted of unfitness, and go forth from the Master's Presence, ashamed and unanswered.

I attended a meeting some time ago in which the moderator opened the meeting by saying, "As we begin, I want to ask the preacher to say a little prayer." Friends, there is no such thing as a *"little prayer"*! If it reaches God, it has a magnitude beyond description; if it doesn't reach God, it isn't a prayer at all.

The words of Christ forbid unsuitable prayer, but that ministry is negative and will only produce a sterile blank if it does not lead to a correction. *The words of Christ should also stir the heart with enlarging desires* for the possession of those good things which Christ has promised to them that love Him. Then prayer becomes a dialogue between the Master who says, "Seek ye my face," and the sensitive spiritual disciple who responds, "Thy face, Lord, will I seek" (Psalm 27:8). As you sift your prayers through the sieve of His words, His words will slowly condition your life so that your prayers will agree with Him — and He will agree with your prayers.

V. SERVE OTHERS IN LOVE, EXPECTING DIVINE FRUIT TO RESULT

Finally, if my prayers are to be favorably heard, and answered, then I must *serve others in love, expecting Divine fruit to result from the service.* Jesus said, "I appointed you that you should go and bring forth fruit, and that your fruit should remain: that whatsoever ye shall ask of the Father in my name, He may give it you" (John 15:16). In other words, answers to prayer will depend very largely (much more than we think) on our ministry to others. You see, it is the sign of a maturing Christian that the focus of his attention and action is increasingly on others, and not merely on himself. I saw a desk motto which read, "No turtle ever moves forward as long as he is enclosed within his shell." No Christian should expect to have his prayers answered as long as he remains imprisoned in the shell of self.

A Christian came upon a fellow believer from behind and startled him. The startled one exclaimed, "You almost made me jump out of my skin!" The other replied, "That just might be a good thing!" Lillian Smith, in her book, <u>The Killers of a Dream</u>, says that there are two journeys every believer must make. One, into himself, should lead him to accept, confess, and surrender what he finds there. The other, into the world, should lead him to regard it as the workshop of his service for Christ. Paul Tournier said essentially the same thing when he wrote, "Every Christian needs two conversions: one out of the world and one back into it." The Christian simply must move beyond personal piety to a consuming concern for other people all over the world. We live in a consumer society, and tragically, the church has often been turned into a consumer community, but where is the Christian who is willing to be consumed — for the glory of God and the good of others?

> "Only two philosophies occupy life's shelf;
> Either live *for God and others*, or you will live *for self.*"

Recently, I read the challenging life-story of William Wilberforce, the little hunchbacked Englishman who led the fight to free the slaves throughout the British Empire. The drama of the story is greatly heightened when we realize that slavery was at the very foundation of the economy of England at the time. When the struggle was most intense, and Wilberforce was showing physical signs of his part in the battle, a friend asked him, "William, how is it with your soul?" Wilberforce, who was spurred on by his marvelous Christian faith, replied, "I forgot that I had a soul." He meant that he had become so absorbed in ministering to others that he had forgotten himself. What a picture of Jesus' statement, "He who would save his life shall lose it, but whoever would lose his life for my sake and the Gospel's, shall save it." To be a healthy human being, according to Jesus, is to exist "between give and take" (or perhaps the proper order is "take and give"). However, we must be sure that the taking is a reception of God's resources, and the giving is a transmission of those resources to others, producing Biblical "fruit."

A wise Christian will hold himself accountable with this question: Do I live in a house of mirrors (always seeing and pampering myself), or in a house of windows (seeing others and ministering to them)? Many of us need to immediately replace our mirrors with windows. We need to balance the "outside-in" living of constant intake, with a suitable "inside-out" ministry of equally constant output. We need to focus on giving until giving matches getting in our lives. We need to change to the mentality of service instead of selfishness, to contribution and not mere acquisition.

"Self is the only prison that can ever bind the soul,
Love is the only angel who can bid the gates unroll;
And when he comes to call thee, arise and follow fast;
His way may lie through darkness, but it leads to life at last."

Many years ago, when Albert Schweitzer visited America, his journey took him to the city of Chicago. He was greeted there by a committee of prominent Chicago citizens, as well as by a great crowd of reporters at the railroad station. Schweitzer suddenly dismissed himself, pressed through the crowd, and helped a struggling little old lady with her baggage. When he returned to his welcoming crowd, he said wryly, "Sorry to keep you waiting, gentlemen, but I was just having my daily fun." A reporter later wrote, "That was the first time I ever saw a sermon walking." Whether that would qualify as "fruit unto God" is surely debatable, but the action and the attitude were unquestionably right. We must serve — for Christ's sake and for the sake of others — and we must get far enough in that service that it becomes the greatest fun of our lives.

Let me repeat this last test: According to Jesus, answers to prayer depend very largely on our ministry to others. If we are prompted by desire for our own comfort, peace, enjoyment, or advantage, we will have a poor chance of receiving answers from Him in prayer. If, on the other hand, our prayers are connected with our fruit-bearing (that is, prayer is for the purpose of bearing "fruit unto God," and the "fruit unto God" is thus merely the extension of our prayers), the golden scepter will be extended to us, as King Ahasuerus extended it to Queen Esther, saying, "What is your request? Even to the half of the kingdom it shall be granted."

When pastor Wallace Bassett was in the central American nation of Panama, he visited the Panama Canal. "Imagine my surprise," he later said, "when I was told that I could lift one of the great ships that pass through the canal." "How am I to do that?" I asked. "Just press this button," was the reply. When Dr. Bassett pressed the specified button, the great canal lock closed and filled with water, lifting the ship in it to the next level. Dr. Bassett remarked, "What a picture of prayer! Prayer is the Divinely-given means for weak believers like myself to elevate Heaven's great causes among men, and to lift life's great and crushing loads." In light of the vast needs, opportunities and responsibilities of today, could any believer make a more strategic contribution than to join with other believers in concentrated prayer?

What is the conclusion of the matter? Simply this: the temple of prayer is guarded from the intrusion of the unprepared footstep by several crucial tests. At the very door, we are challenged by the watchword: *Seek the glory of God alone.* If our lives do not harmonize with God's glory, we are allowed to go no further. Then, the key that unlocks the door is *engraved with the name of Jesus. Submit your prayers to the standard of Christ's character.* The locked door to the Audience-chamber will only open to the hand in which His nature is pulsating. Then, we must *stay in obedient union with Him.* We must abide in Him and He in us if He is to plead in and through us. Then, His words must monitor and monopolize our lives if our prayers are to be answered. And finally, we must *serve others in love, expecting Divine fruit to result from the service.* It is as we serve our Master according to His orders that we can count absolutely on His answer to our prayers.

As we accept and apply and act upon the mandates given by these "tests," we can expect that prayer will become ever more engrossing and rewarding. We will discover the door of the prayer closet to be the little door that opens to The Largest Life. May God help us to keep the hinges of that door well-oiled and the Throne-room well-visited! Go into the Holy of Holies, spread His Book open before the Mercy Seat and between you and Him, wait until the Shekinah ("Presence") Light shines upon its sacred page, and when you have had an audience with the King and caught His pulse beat, rise to go out and serve in His name. Surprising fruit will be the result.

Chapter 11

REMEMBER -- AND BE THANKFUL

(Deuteronomy 8)

"All the commandments that I am commanding you today you shall be careful to do, that you may live and multiply, and go in and possess the land which the LORD swore to give to your forefathers. And you shall remember all the way which the LORD your God has led you in the wilderness these forty years, that He might humble you, testing you, to know what was in your heart whether you would keep His commandments or not."

I want to base this study on just three words of the text: *"...You shall REMEMBER..."*. The text takes us into the wilderness wanderings of the children of Israel before God takes them into the promised land. In the text, God states three reasons, three Divine motives, for leading His people in the wilderness for forty years. God's stated reasons were: (1) To "humble you". Our English word "humble" comes from the Latin word *humous* (from which we derive such words as "human" and "humor"!), which means "dirt," or "soil," or "earth." So God intended His people to be brought all the way down to their mother element ("dust thou art and to dust thou shalt return") as a part of their desert training. (2) To "test you." God intended to expose the character of His people, hoping to show their complete genuineness, but willing also to show any lack of genuineness so that the lack might be corrected. (3) "To know what was in your heart, whether you would keep His commandments or not." So God suspended His people on His Word, to humble, test and expose them. "To know what was in your heart" does not mean that God intended to learn the truth about them. God is omniscient, which also includes foreknowledge. He already knows everything, including the heart of His people (each one). So this testing was to reveal to His people what was in their hearts—to encourage their faith and correct their faithlessness.

I want to call your particular attention to the three words mentioned above: *"You shall remember."* What a season of the year to "recall"! What a season of the year to remember! Is your life like mine? I'm now approaching the end of my third quarter of a century of life. I never thought I'd make it this far! I'm like the guy who said, "I guess if I knew I was going to live this long I would've taken better care of myself!" Human life is like having a smooth rope in your hands, and it seems to run smoothly through your hands without interruption, and you look up here and it's Sunday again. And then you look up there and it's the first of the month again. And, you look up ahead and the big calendar days are coming around again. Christmas is gone, and Thanksgiving preceded it. Quick as a flash, they are both gone. We have just hurriedly turned the corner into a new year. Time is running through your life (or your life is running through time) as if it were in a terrible hurry. Now, aren't you glad that our calendar, which was framed partially out of the Christian understanding, has days on it in a year's time that are like tying knots in that rope. So, while it is smoothly flowing through your hands you are reminded occasionally that it's not going slowly. Time is moving very rapidly and if you are wise, you will at least occasionally stop and take your bearings. New Year's is one of those days. I'm so glad that somebody had wisdom enough to suggest that I stop and take my bearings about God and all spiritual realities and blessings, and that I again state my appreciation of everything God has been to me and done for me. What should I think of—and thank God for—near the beginning of a new year?

Our text calls us to exercise the ministry of *memory*. Memory is such a peculiar thing. It is the only way you can learn. All the learning you have in your mind is a matter of memory. It's a vast storage chest. Every day things are being deposited in your memory. It's the only way the past can live again in life as we have it right now. Author James Berry said, "Memory is God's way of giving us roses in the month of December."

Memory is a strange thing. There is an Independent Baptist preacher named Jack Van Impe, who has memorized the entire New Testament. He has done this so he can pronounce the word of God at anytime simply by mental recall. During his lifetime, the late Southern Baptist Evangelist Angel Martinez could quote the entire New Testament, and then he proceeded to learn it in Greek! Do you suppose that in Heaven he is now quoting it in Hebrew? Just a thought.

Memory is indeed a strange, wonderful gift. You see, we are so endowed that we can have immediate *tragedy* in our minds through memory. The memory of most persons in this room right now is a "bondslave". When you look back over your past, in memory, what do you tend to focus on? Let me just confess for most of us. The memory of many is a bondslave to *dirt*! When looking back over our past, most of us tend to focus on some *dirty* spot on the page of memory.

The national media has had much to say in recent years concerning the treasures of King Tut and King Ramses II of Egypt, and those are fabulous treasures. When I was in Cairo, Egypt, I was privileged to visit the national museum there. I saw the many related treasures of these two Egyptian kings, and they are indeed fabulous. Each of these Kings was buried in a gold sarcophagus *(somebody said, "Man, that's REAL living")*. Did you know that the Egyptians not only embalmed Kings and Queens, *but they embalmed rats and cats too!* Well, that's the way our memories are. We can draw out *Kings and Queens*, or we can draw out *cats and rats. Which do we (I) tend to easily draw out of our (my) memory?* We must candidly confess that we too easily draw out the cats and the rats. We look back and many of our memories are bondslaves to the dirt in our past, though our past may through the grace of God be overwhelmed by *His cleansing..* But we still morbidly tend to major on the dirt. Isn't that interesting? That's part of our *depravity*.

Then, our memories may be the bondslaves of *disappointment*. What do you tend to major on when you look back on your past? Your mind may focus on something in the past which you can't forgive, whether a circumstance of life or a wrong that was done to you. Your expectation was frustrated by an undesirable replacement, and you have had a tough time forgetting it. Whatever it was, you tend to look at dirt and/or disappointment in your past, and thus violate the best use of the gift of memory. That's not to say that those things are unimportant, but they should be settled so that they don't command your attention. There's the tragedy of memory.

Think now of the good side of memory. One of the good things about your memory is that it can be trained. That is surely one of the reasons we are commanded in our text to remember. We (each of us) have the option (once we realize it) to turn our memory in a desirable, even Divine, direction. David said, "Therefore will I remember You. I will remember God" (Psalm 42:6). Wherefore the "therefore"? Among other things, it means we can train our memory. We can look back over certain things that cause our memory to be turned toward God and train our memory to focus on those things—and on Him.

In Lamentations 3:21, Jeremiah said, "This I recall to mind, therefore I have hope." That is, because I can deliberately choose to recall this to mind, therefore I have hope.

Victor Frankl wrote a little book entitled <u>A Search For Meaning</u>. In it he tells how he was confined in a Nazi concentration camp. The Nazi camp officials thought they took *everything* away from him. They stripped the last thread of clothes from his body. They shaved his head, his facial hair, and every other hair on his body. They stripped him of everything and forced him to stand totally exposed in a line of people who were in the same condition. He said, "I lost it all, and I wondered what I had to protect or preserve. I had no dignity and apparently little identity. *But then I realized that I had one very valuable thing left—they could not take away my ability to choose my reaction to what they did to me.*" You see, at that awful moment, Victor Frankl commanded his memory to attention, dictated to it what he wanted to draw from the storehouse—and therefore he had hope. What a tremendous thing memory is!

Did you know that the renowned British Prime Minister of the past, Sir Winston Churchill, who was a rotund cigar-smoking politician, was an amiable genius? When he was a young pre-teen he won a memory contest by quoting 1200 lines of McCauley's book of history on ancient Rome!

Daniel Webster, a great political name in the national history of the United States, once won a Sunday School scripture memory contest by quoting a dozen chapters of the Bible. When the teacher declared the contest over and declared him the winner, he got angry because he had another dozen chapters he was going to recite! The human memory is a fantastic thing! We are even told that we only use one percent of the potential of our memories regardless of how we employ them. But they can be trained.

In the chapter that contains our text, God is inviting us to focus our memories on at least four different things. Each of these is included in a larger focus, a focus on God. Let me isolate these four things and briefly address them.

I. God's DELIVERANCE

First, Moses tells his people to remember *God's Deliverance.* Look at verse 14 of this eighth chapter of Deuteronomy. "Then your heart becomes proud and you forget the LORD your God Who brought you out from the land of Egypt, out of the house of slavery." Moses is referring here to the focal point of deliverance in all of Jewish history. It's impossible for us, at this late day in history, to truly understand and realize what that means to a Jew. That 14th verse points to a landmark day on the national calendar of Israel, the Jewish National Birthday! It was on that day that the Jews' calendar began. Are you aware of that? On that day of deliverance the Jewish calendar was totally changed to accommodate that date as the greatest day, up to that point, in Jewish history!

Look at Deuteronomy 16:3 and you will see this date etched firmly in the word of God. In that passage, Moses is stating some of the specifications for some of the national feasts of Israel, and he says, "You shall not eat leavened bread with it; seven days you shall eat with it unleavened bread, the bread of affliction (for you came out of the land of Egypt in haste), *in order that you may remember* all the days of your life *the day* when you came out of the land of Egypt." (emphasis mine)

Now, think about your own personal history. What is the greatest day of deliverance that has ever come to you? Is not the day of your salvation through Jesus Christ the greatest day of deliverance you have ever known? The Christian calendar documents that in an easy way. It has in it a B.C. (before Christ) and an A.D. (Ano Dommini--the year of our Lord) that splits history asunder by the coming of Jesus. But this date is not merely a date in *history*; it has a counterpart in your *heart*. Now *you* have a "B.C." also. Stop just now and remember what it was like during that "B.C." time. When you were dead in trespasses and sins, what was it like? When you were shackled to a master who was forcing upon you a horrible slavery, look back for a moment and try to remember, what was it like? When Satan had his foot on your neck and lorded it over you, and you had no choice to do anything else but obey him. You were in darkness, under your Pharaoh, in the bondage of Satan, sin, and the world. You had no choice to do anything else, until God broke in with His light to offer you His life. Then came *the* day, the beginning of your "A.D." history. Let your memory focus on that incredible mercy of God!

In the New Testament, anytime you see the word "saved", or any other form of that word, you can rightly replace it with the word "*delivered*". A Christian is one who has been "DELIVERED". This is one of the most neglected doctrines in all of scripture, and as a result, many are confused as to what truly constitutes being a Christian. One of the great words in the Bible is the word "deliverance." It is, however, not commonly used in the Christian vocabulary. I don't recall in my life ever having heard but one sermon which defined God's salvation as eternal deliverance. I don't recollect that in any part of the world where I have talked with Christians who speak my language that they have used the word "deliverance" unless it has been used in some context related to demons, or exorcism. The word "deliverance" is not a common word of Christian vocabulary, but it really should be. The fact that it isn't is a serious failure on our part because the word opens to us a category of truth that pointedly clarifies God's redemptive purpose. In Psalm 91 God is seen three times as the Deliverer who will deliver His people. In fact, "deliverance" may be the best, it may be the most comprehensive, and it may be the most clarifying word to explain God's gracious powerful work in our lives in saving us.

The word "deliverance" is a great word biblically, and it's a great word in the English language. We all understand the English word "deliverance." In fact, that word has in it a certain tone of adventure, doesn't it? There's a certain drama in the word "deliverance." In the English language, a good synonym for "deliverance" is the word, "rescued". When we think of deliverance we may think of somebody being rescued out of a situation of grave danger. And that is what the word does in fact mean. It connotes somebody in an impossible dilemma from which they don't have personally the power to extract themselves, and yet somehow they are rescued by some great person or power. And when we go to the Bible, that's exactly what we find when the word "deliverance" is used.

Biblically, the word "deliverance" is a rich word. In the Old Testament there are three Hebrew words that are translated "deliver." The first is *natsal* and it essentially means "to rescue or to deliver." It is used of physical rescue or physical deliverance. For example, God says in Exodus 3:8, "I have come down to deliver Israel." That is, I came down to rescue them, to bring them out of the land of Egypt, into a good and spacious land, the land of Canaan. So God came to rescue, to deliver in a dramatic and adventurous way the children of Israel out of Egyptian bondage and take them into the land of promise. The word *natsal* is used of that kind of literal, physical deliverance and rescue.

Natsal is also used numerous times to speak of spiritual deliverance. It is so used on a number of occasions *in the Psalms...Psalm 39:8; Psalm 51:14; Psalm 69:14; Psalm 79:9 and other passages use the* word *natsal* to refer to some kind of spiritual rescue, rescuing the sinner from judgment, from sin, etc.

Secondly, there is the word *palat*. That word is a synonym to *natsal*, it means "to save or deliver." It is used in the Old Testament in several poetic passages. In fact, it is limited to usages in Old Testament poetry. So you find it very, very often in the Psalms, as well as a few other times in other places where poetry is included in the Old Testament. It again describes deliverance, and one commentator said that it could be translated "escape."

There is a third word, *yasha*, and it is the most common word. It means "to deliver, or to save, or rescue." It is translated by the word "save" in most incidences where it occurs.

Any of those words carries the same idea, the idea of a rescue, the idea of a dramatic deliverance for someone who is in a dangerous situation over which they have not sufficient control. And usually when these words are used in the Old Testament, God is the Deliverer and man is the delivered, God is the Rescuer and man is the rescued. So one of the great concepts in the Old Testament is this concept of deliverance. God is the Deliverer, man is the delivered, and God is the one who also provides the plan of deliverance. When you come to the New Testament, nothing changes. You go from the Hebrew language to the Greek language from which the New Testament was written and you find a familiar word in the New Testament, *sozo*. That word is usually translated "save, saved, or salvation." And it means to be rescued, or to be delivered. In fact, when the New Testament mentions salvation, or being saved, most often it uses the word *sozo*. It can mean a physical rescue, it can mean an actual rescue of a person from a dangerous earthly situation, but most often it has to do with deliverance from spiritual danger. One of our great hymns echoes this great truth:

> "Jesus sought me when a stranger,
> Wandering from the fold of God;
> He, to rescue me from danger,
> Interposed His precious blood."

There's a second Greek word, *rhuomai*, used some eighteen times in the New Testament, which means the same thing, to deliver or to rescue. Paul uses that word in Colossians 1:13 when he says, "God has delivered us from the domain of darkness into the kingdom of His dear or beloved Son." So there are two New Testament words and three Old Testament words, all of which deal with this concept of being delivered...being rescued...being taken out of a dangerous predicament and put into a better situation. Deliverance then, by all accounts, is a crucial Biblical idea. It is unfortunate that this concept has been smothered under familiar terminology, most often the well-worn terms, "being saved" and "salvation". In the community of believers, these words have been casually used so often that they are like much-handled coins whose image and superscription have been dimmed by the handling. In fact, it would seem that we rarely use the word "saved" in common speech unless we're talking about something that's put away for safe keeping, like a savings account which contains money which the owner is holding back for future usage. We don't use the word "saved" for the most part to speak of being rescued from danger.

Psalm 68:20 says, "God is to us a God of deliverances." Note the use of the plural form. There are many facets to God as our Deliverer. Psalm 40:17 says, "Thou art my help and my Deliverer, O my God." Psalm 144:1,2 adds, "Blessed be the Lord my rock, my lovingkindness, my fortress, my stronghold and my Deliverer." This will help us emphasize what salvation really is, it is deliverance. When a sinner is born again, he is instantly delivered from a certain very dangerous and deadly predicament, a predicament that was posing an imminent fatal danger to his eternal soul. True salvation then, a miracle work of God, is deliverance. It is the dramatic rescue of the sinner from the elements of life that threaten to destroy him now and damn him forever.

How our remembrance of this personal deliverance should arouse our hearts to thankfulness and celebration! Speaking of this deliverance, Jesus said in John 5:24, "In that day you passed out of (literally, 'migrated from') death into life." It is as if you went through a doorway out of darkness and into God's light, then closed the door behind you on all the darkness and death of the past. You were suddenly, eternally, fully, finally, freely and forever delivered! In our text, God is asking us to do the obvious: remember that deliverance.

II. God's GUIDANCE

Second, we are asked in Deuteronomy 8 to remember *God's guidance.* "God's Guidance"—what full words those are! Look at the first phrases of Deuteronomy 8:2. "And you shall remember all the way…"— God's guidance is *full* guidance ; "…which the LORD your God led you…"— God's guidance is *factual* (actual) guidance.

Focus your attention on the word, "remember." The meaning of that word is, literally, "to mark." Imagine a roadmap in your mind. Now, use that roadmap to trace the many winding paths you have traveled in your past. That map is like a chart in your mind. As you chart your past travels on the map, put an asterisk beside those certain places, occurrences and events in your past where you are especially conscious of God's guidance. Personally, my map has some giant landmarks on it!

Let me emphasize the illustration. Your past should look in your memory like a road map on which a trip has been charted (was it actually planned by Someone Else?). When you look back at all the varying occurrences in your past, you can see by the asterisks in your mind, all along the way, though you could not fully understand at the time, that "the LORD your God led you all the way."

There is an important lesson here for a Christian. You see, the Children of Israel didn't even want to consider their wilderness wanderings as a part of their deliverance. They wanted to leave Egypt and make a quick and easy trip to the Promised Land. But God sovereignly and strategically led them to and through the wilderness. At times when they were at their lowest, God was leading them, conditioning them, testing them and pushing them into the channels of His guidance *and grace* all the way. He was always guiding them.

Dear Christian, the same is true of you on your Homeward journey. It will likely include travel through a wilderness, and one day you will fully celebrate His plan in taking you through it.

Samuel Logan Bringle wrote several meaningful Christian books. The writing of his first book is a remarkable testimony of the guidance of God. Bringle graduated with honors from Harvard University. He was seriously offered a prestigious diplomatic post with the United States Government, and was highly qualified to fulfill the responsibility of the position. Instead, he turned the post down to join the street ministry of the Salvation Army. He went out on the street to love needy people in Christ's Name and to preach Christ to lost sinners. Through his faithfulness he was given the title and position of "Colonel" in the Salvation Army. Bringle routinely led Salvation Army "soldiers" onto the streets to preach Christ. He was singing and preaching with some of the soldiers on a street corner in Brooklyn, New York, one day, when an aimless bum who was staggering drunk came stumbling down the sidewalk. The pitiful man apparently had an allergic (carnal) reaction to the proclamation of Christ. As the preacher was preaching, the bum picked up a brick and aimlessly hurled it toward the crowd of Salvation Army soldiers, and it struck Samuel Bringle on the head and knocked him unconscious. He had a severe concussion, and as a result of complications from it, he spent the next seven months recovering in a hospital. Much later in his life, with developed hindsight, he wrote these words, "I thought that act was a total violation of everything I hoped and intended for my ministry." However, he wrote his first little book while he was laid up recovering in the hospital. When he saw how immediately prominent the book became, he soon wrote four others, each equally popular. Those books are sold by the tens of thousands even today. He said, "I guess you could say God's providence in my life could be described by the formula, *No brick, no book!"*

Every one of us has had agonizing moments, moments which have challenged our faith and our faithfulness. But this is the way God works. Jesus once said, "Even so, Father, for so it seemed good in Your sight." This should be a motto verse for us in such moments. The "book" will never be "written" unless the Divinely-thrown "brick" strikes us on/in the head.

"Our crosses will come from different trees,
But we must all have our Calvaries."

The Apostle Paul often said that he longed to go to Rome to minister in his Master's Name—but he never thought he would go in chains! When Paul was imprisoned and taken in chains to Rome, he thought his ministry was over, but Caesar's household was impacted through his imprisonment, and the ends of the earth began to hear about Christ, and Christians were encouraged by Paul's faithfulnesss while in a Roman jail awaiting execution. When we look back over the roadmap of memory, we are to celebrate the guidance of God.

III. God's PROVIDENCE

Third, we are to remember *God's providence.* This truth is closely related to the other two points. We are to remember God's *Deliverance*, which is a part of His *Providence*, and we are to remember God's *guidance*, which is also a part of His providence. Then, in a much larger way, we are to remember God's providence itself.

Look at Deuteronomy 8:5. Here we will see a significant part of God's providence. Here is a negative providence with a positive purpose. "Thus you are to know in your heart (another term for memory) that the LORD your God was disciplining you just as a man disciplines his son. Therefore you shall keep the commandments of the LORD your God, to walk in His ways and to fear Him." As we read further, think of this against the background of American blessings and benefits. "For the LORD your God is bringing you into a good land, a land of brooks of water, of fountains and springs, flowing forth in valleys and hills; a land of wheat and barley, of vines and fig trees and pomegranates, a land of olive oil *and honey, a land where you shall eat food without scarcity,*(could anything be a better portrait of our national history than this?) in which you shall not lack anything; a land whose stones are iron,(in other words it will have plenty of natural resources) and out of whose hills you can dig copper."

Now, look at verse 18. Here is the second of three radically different aspects of God's Providence. One is negative. One is positive, and one is personal. The others wouldn't do us any good if it weren't for this personal one. "But you shall remember the LORD your God, for it is HE Who is giving you power to make wealth (so it is God Who endows you with the ability to make money) in order that He may establish His covenant which He swore to your fathers, as it is this day."

The text clearly says that God has provided three basic things. Let me reverse the order. First, He has provided prosperity (verses 7-9). We often have a strange depraved tendency when we begin to enjoy His prosperity. We often forget God as if we voted deliberately to do so. That's why He says, "Lest you forget..."

The pastor of a Baptist Church stepped to the pulpit to make announcements one Sunday, and as he did, someone passed him a note. He read the note silently, then with downcast look he announced that the church needed to pray for

"Brother John" because a great crisis had just come into his life. After the service was concluded, a few of the members asked the pastor if he could divulge the nature of the crisis. He responded that a wealthy relative of Brother John's had just died and bequeathed a fortune to Brother John. He further stated that was a bigger crisis than if Brother John had just lost a fortune, because now he would have to adjust to the stewardship of prosperity, and the natural tendency is for the person to forget God.

Our nation is presently building a history of such stewardship abuse, and if it continues, God will exercise the providence of severe discipline. That seems to be the only way we will pay any attention to reality again. We're not going to give Him adequate attention as long as we in our depravity choose to forget Him, when God has given us all of these things.

Second, God has provided personal capacity and capability to each of us. Every positive capacity I have is like an empty spot placed in me by God to be filled with the blessings He gives as I cooperate with Him in developing these capacities. It is amazing to see how we in these favored United States have developed a "myth of independence". We've vaunted ourselves as an independent people. I occasionally meet somebody who arrogantly says, "I am a man of independence. I am a self-made man. I have independent means." The truth is, we're not even independent of nature! Just look at what has happened in recent years on the world scene with the Tsunami, the Florida hurricanes of 2004 and 2005, and then the recent Hurricane Katrina tragedy. When a natural tragedy strikes us, many rally to the point of need, but we can't control the natural occurrence itself. My house could be gone today! My earthly possessions could be snatched away today! The "myth" of independence is just exactly that. We're very dependent on a world neighborhood. Let a terrorist organization or a rogue Third World country develop nuclear capability and you will realize how true this is. God has His own subtle back-door ways of enforcing our dependence. This has been proven in history over and over again, and it is obvious to anyone who has an eye open to that reality. God has provided us personal capacity and capability.

Third, God has provided us with adversity. Deuteronomy 8:2 says, "…the Lord your God who chastened you…" Every adverse thing that comes my way is actually a provision of God, at least in a backdoor way. Does Romans 8:28 say, "God causes all *good* things to work together for good to those who love God, to those who are the called according to His purpose"? *NO!!!* It rightly states, "God causes *all things* to work together for good to those who love God…" (emphasis mine)

I look at it this way. My life has two uncertain ingredients, one called prosperity and the other called adversity. I love the prosperity that God sends, but the adversity is just as necessary at any time. In fact, God may almost laugh when he brings adversity into my personal history. And one day, when He makes all things clear, we will laugh with Him. Incidentally, I saw a Family Circle cartoon recently in which the two little girls were in church. The pastor was in the pulpit with finger raised (the stance of preaching, I guess). One of the girls is saying to the other, "Did you hear what he said? He said, 'Everybody in Heaven has ever-laughing life." They really do!

The book (and subsequent movie) entitled *Daddy Longlegs* is the story of a very poor girl in an orphanage. She had no resources to get out. She was kept two years beyond the normal termination point because she had no means to survive once she got out. "Daddy Longlegs" is the affectionate name she gives to a man, a millionaire, who came to the orphanage one day (she didn't even see him) and adopted an orphan. The one they gave to him was this girl. As the years passed he anonymously sponsored her financially. He underwrote all of her expenses for necessities and luxuries. And when she went to the office and asked who did these things, they told her it was an unknown benefactor. One day, however, she caught a glimpse of him disappearing into his nice luxury car. All she saw was the silhouette of his body. He was long and tall, and she saw him in the late evening sun and his body cast a long shadow that made her think of a "daddy long legs" spider. So she began to correspond with him, though her correspondence was one-way. The book is made up largely of letters that she wrote to the man she called "Daddy Longlegs". If you have read the story or seen the movie, you will remember that some years later she had become a very skilled, educated, attractive, beautiful young woman, and she finally met him. When she met him, she fell in love with him.

Do you see the underlying analogy here? Every one of us has a Benefactor far more capable, far bigger, and far wealthier than we know or consider. All we see are the suggestions of His existence (like the shadows in the story). We don't see Him visually, but He has underwritten our existence—our physical needs, our "education", our providential needs, our finances, etc.—throughout our lives. The tragedy is, that as we try to look through the veil of uncertainty in examining Who this is Who is doing all these things for us, most of us seldom become like the girl in the story. Most people are too selfish to satisfactorily investigate and meet that unknown Benefactor. They just assume they deserve all of these blessings. *I'm the beneficiary of Somebody I've never seen, but I have been introduced to Him and I know Him.* He has underwritten my entire life, and I don't mind telling you that *since I've come to know Him, I deeply and dearly love Him*!

You see, God presides over us even when we don't know it is happening. In time, He spells out the dimensions of His Sponsorship so that we can begin to correspond with Him (actually, we read His correspondence to us) and if we are wise, we actually come to know Him, and love Him. Have you detected Him yet? Have you met Him yet? Have you fallen in love with Him yet?

Some years ago, I read Victor Hugo's great novel, <u>Les Miserables.</u> I think it is the greatest single novel I have ever read. Though this is not pertinent to the actual plot of the story, the book contains an absolutely masterful description of the Battle of Waterloo, the famous battle in which the Duke of Wellington defeated the French forces of Napoleon. It traces the military movements and shows how, by every apparent consideration, the forces of Napoleon should have won the battle. Let me repeat a few words from the book itself.

"Had it not rained on the night of the 17th of June 1815, the future of Europe would have been totally changed. A few drops of water more or less prostrated Napoleon. That Waterloo should be the end of Napoleon's attempt to rule the world, providence needed only a few drops of rain, and an unseasonable cloud crossing the sky sufficed for the overthrow of the world. Had the ground been dry and the artillery able to move the action would've commenced at 6:00 in the morning. The battle would've been won and finished at 2:00 in the afternoon– 3 hours before the Prussian force arrived and turned the scale of fortune in favor of Wellington and his army.

"On the night of the 17th of June, Napoleon made fun of Wellington. 'This little Englishman must have his lesson'.

The rain doubled. It thundered while the Emperor was speaking. Napoleon had been impeached before the court of the infinite God, and his fall was decreed. The fact is, he vexed God. Waterloo is not a mere battle. It is the change of the countenance of the universe.

"Had the action commenced 2 hours earlier, it would've been finished at 4:00, and Blucker (the German General) would've fallen upon a field already won by Napoleon. Such are these immense chances apportioned to an infinity which we cannot grasp." In other words, it appears that Providence made one ploy after another to neutralize and negate Napoleon and assure victory to Wellington. Listen again. Let me abbreviate one aspect in my own words: Napoleon had taken his command post for the battle upon a knoll. He had to delay his attack until 11:00 – five hours beyond the time he had originally appointed, because his artillery was mired in the mud from the rain. When he commanded his army to attack, they charged across the battlefield only to encounter something that Napoleon with all of his military genius had not seen. There was a chasm about 30 feet wide all the way across the battlefield, but from a distance Napoleon and his officers had not seen it. So they came thundering across that battlefield to make the first thrust at the French, but they saw the chasm too late, and they drove their first 4 lines of cavalrymen into the chasm and trampled them so that the rest of them were forced to stumble over the horses and bodies of their own army.

This is a classic report of God's Providence in history. This happens all the time, in large scale and small, nationally and personally, and we don't know it. It is a major matter of providence that I did not die of cancer yesterday, or have a car accident that snuffed out my life. But I take this for granted because I did not think of such preventive blessings.

In a million different ways, God presides over our lives in His providence. He does all things well, and He doesn't even consult us!

IV. God's PATIENCE

Finally, we are to remember *God's patience.* Twice in the opening verses of Deuteronomy 8, the text says, "...the LORD your God led you in the wilderness these forty years..." Remember how Hebrews says it: "They provoked Him for forty years in the wilderness." Look also at Deuteronomy 9:7, where we will see the very word that is used in reporting this story in the New Testament book of Hebrews: "Remember and do not forget how you provoked the LORD your God to wrath in the wilderness; from the day that you left Egypt until you arrived at this place, you have been rebellious against the LORD."

I wonder if anyone of us has any possible appreciation of how much of what we are as moral human beings, as spiritual creatures, and as Christians, has depended on God's patience. Where would we be without God's patience? The Bible makes it quite clear. It says, "The longsuffering of the Lord is our salvation." Think of that very carefully. God's ability to suffer with us, or to be patient with us for a long time is what accounts for our salvation. If God had only been "just" without mercy, without patience, without longsuffering, we would've been wiped out a long time ago. If God had marked iniquities, who should stand?

As the Children of Israel were under the administration of God's counsel in Deuteronomy chapters 8 and 9, He told them to look back over their days in the wilderness and their days under His administrative authority. When they did so, they were reminded that those days were often filled with evil. They saw patterns of anger. The saw great pockets of rebellion. They looked at the page of memory with disgust as they saw national and personal unbelief. They saw their complaining as a part of their sin. They saw their resentment of God as a part of their sin. I'm sure they wondered why God would remind them of their sins. God said, "Remember and do not forget these things." It wasn't that He would have them brood over the past, or have them worn down with the guilt of the memory of their sins, but they were to remember as reminders of God's patience and mercy. They were to remember how He had forgiven them in spite of their sins. They were to remember how He had blessed them in spite of their sins. They were to remember how He had strengthened them in spite of their sins. To think of their sins was to be reminded of God's mercy and patience.

His biographer tells us that the great evangelist, Gypsy Smith, had mounted on his office desk an old pearl-handled dagger. It was a conversation piece for many people who came to his office. He would explain that it was the dagger his own Grandfather had used to kill more than one person. In other words, he reminded himself by means of the history of sin in his ancestry and his own personal past, of the patience of God in his life.

How do you suppose Simon Peter reacted and responded every time he heard a rooster crow after his denial of Jesus? No doubt he was reminded of the patient mercy of Jesus that had rescued and restored him.

The title of this study is "Remember and Be Thankful." There are two verbs in this title. "Remember" is the first one, and then "Be Thankful" is the verbal action that comes out of the ministry of memory. The word "remember" recurs often in the book of Deuteronomy. It probably is repeated so often because it is so easy to forget. That is one reason we must have preaching and teaching among Christians. Christian memories cannot be trusted, and we must be reminded continually.

Paul wrote to Timothy in II Timothy 2:8, "Remember Jesus Christ risen from the dead, descendant of David, according to my gospel." Now, it is hardly conceivable that Paul or Timothy could forget Christ, but Paul was mindful that without the ministry of memory things are blotted out that we desperately need to retain in our minds.

Think of the name of the book where our text is found. It is the book of "Deuteronomy." Do you know the meaning of that word? It is a compound word that comes from Greek directly into English. It comes from the Greek translation of the Old Testament, called the "Septuagint". *Deutero – Nomos is the word.* "Deutero" means "second" or "repeat". "Nomos" means "law". So, the book of Deuteronomy is a repeat statement of the law of God and God's workings and dealings with His people in the beginning of their national history as Jews. In other words, one statement of the law wasn't enough. One statement of their history with God wasn't enough. They needed consistent and constant reminders of that statement of the law along with amplifications and interpretations of it. They needed constant reminders of their national history with God.

It was Rudyard Kipling who said, "Lord God of Hosts, be with us yet...lest we forget...lest we forget." What an incredible gift of grace your personal memory is! Memory provides the chance for endless mental reruns. It is the faculty that allows us to use time more than once. Memory is a strange blight on the one hand, and a strange blessing on the other hand. Memory is the treasury of thought and the treasurer of the mind. It has been called the library of the mind. It makes earlier joys and events available again. It restores the blessedness of the past, and even provides companionship when you are all alone. It is the guardian of all things in our past that can be called up. Proverbs 10:7 says, "The memory of the just is blessed."

Let me remind you that today will be a memory tomorrow. What kind of memory will it be as you unpack the treasure chest and draw out today's occurrences when tomorrow comes? Let me also remind you that *you* will be a memory to somebody else tomorrow. What kind of memory will you be to the people you are with today when tomorrow comes, or when you are no longer in this world?

Moses knew that memory is a servant of the will. Your will can force your memory to call things up. We are *commanded* to remember and not to forget—so that we can be thankful instead of thoughtless. The grace of God offers among its many gifts the grace of *gratitude* to replace our ingratitude. You see, *ingratitude* is a sin. But "one act of thanksgiving, when things go wrong, is worth a thousand acts of thanksgiving when things go right."

Consider two final truths. First, consider that the only proper response to grace is gratitude. Grace is the roof over everything in the life of the child of God. "Say 'Thank you'" are almost the first words we learn in life, and they are about the last words on life. Objectively, life offers many things that may discontent us and could make us cynical if we allow those things to condition us. One of life's biggest assignments is to drown our discontent in appreciation. We too easily lose the trail blazed by the stars by groveling in the dust and dirt. We can follow that trail by practicing regular thanksgiving.

Second, the one real resource for growth in your life today may be gratitude. If you're stalemated by some circumstance or occurrence that has stifled your thanksgiving, the thing that will set in motion your spiritual growth again is to break into gratitude. *Growth is stalemated, staggered, and stopped by cynicism and ingratitude.* Ingratitude not only poisons the air around you, but it also poisons you. So, when God commands you to Remember and Be Thankful He is doing you and everybody else an incredible service, but the service begins with you. Gratitude not only pleases God, but it frees the grace of God to go on blessing and growing and shaping you. Gratitude will reopen the clogged channel between you and God and allow Him to fill you with His fullness and His blessings today.

Christian…Today…***Remember and Be Thankful!***

Chapter 12

THE PRAYER OF JABEZ

I Chronicles 4:9-10: *"And Jabez was more honorable that his brothers: and his mother called his name Jabez, saying, Because I have him with sorrow. And Jabez called on the God of Israel, saying, Oh that You would bless me indeed, and enlarge my coast, and that Your hand might be with me, and that You would keep me from evil, that it might not grieve me! And God granted him that which he requested."*

This is both an exemplary text and an exceptional text. It is *exemplary* in that these requests of Jabez are the most consistent appeals that the God of Heaven receives from the most people—we could say, from the "average" human being. However, most such prayers today are essentially self-centered and selfish, selfish enough to thoroughly disqualify the prayer even from a hearing in Heaven, and surely from receiving a favorable answer from God.

The average pray-er's "prayer list" looks like a self-oriented grocery list of personal concerns. Without question, God is reluctant to hear and answer a prayer that is as loaded with "me" as an opera singer's rehearsal (there are five usages of "me" and "my" in Jabez' one-verse prayer!). But the prayer of Jabez is *exceptional*. There surely is an exception in this prayer, though no explanation is give. This is *often God's way*! He does not feel it necessary to explain Himself, though He likely expects us to pursue His Way until we have a measure of His reasoning in understanding that Way. Why does God show exceptional favor to this exemplary prayer? In order for us to understand it, this text must stand alone and receive an unbiased treatment. Unbiased, but how so? We must recognize that God is never inconsistent with Himself, that if He regards Jabez with favor, the prayer must be interpreted according to the character of God. So let's see if we can arrive at a view that honors both the character of God and the claim of Jabez.

We begin by acknowledging that there was a city in Judah (southern Israel) named Jabez (see I Chronicles 2:55), and we must admit that it may have been named after this man. If so, he was not as unknown and unrecognized in his own contemporary culture and time as he is to us today.

So here is a fascinating Biblical portrait of a man, attended by a biographical statement that is equally fascinating. What can we learn about him and his relationship with God?

I. The Appearance of Jabez

First, let me briefly note *his appearance* in this long (*long!*) genealogical section of the Word of God. I doubt that you could easily read the long, long genealogical lists that fill the book of First Chronicles. But you should at least read carefully the entire monotonous section in which this text is found and see the flood of names. Note also that the many other people who are mentioned in the section are apparently included basically because of their social and inter-relational

The Prayer of Jabez

lives with others in their contemporary culture, but Jabez is mentioned primarily *because of his relationship with God*. The lesson? Of course, social relationships are important. Of course, interpersonal relatedness is important in the human race. We are "thrown together in the mix of life", and it is incumbent upon each of us to favorably relate to our fellow men.

Alexander Pope once sadly bemoaned "man's inhumanity to his fellow man," and surely there is a plethora of such inhuman and inhumane treatment among men to mourn. But the Relational God has made man for gracious and good relationships with others! Jesus summarized the Mind of God when He said, "The first and greatest commandment is this: You shall love the Lord your God with all of your heart, mind, soul and strength; and the second is like unto it, You shall love your neighbor as yourself." Man, being out of sorts with God, has placed himself in lifelong contest with *God*, often in erratic conflict with his *neighbor*, and uneasily out of sorts with *himself*. You see, there is really no glory for man without God. The elusiveness of the Utopia that man seeks independently of God will *always* embarrass his misdirected ambition and arrogance. So we would be wise to learn God's lessons from the exceptional portrait of Jabez included briefly in this too-regular list of names.

The scribe who wrote the long list of names had a weary task—just names. Ah, but when he arrived at this name he was so deeply (and Divinely) impressed by the consistent honor and holiness of Jabez, that when he inscribes his name, he forgets the usual form of name only, and he records not just a name, but a "character", a fully-formed and true human being.

The portrait of Jabez in this long monotonous section of mere names is like a star set in the darkness of midnight.

His name is a rehearsal of greatness riveted in a chronicle of largely insignificant people. The rule holds, "If any man love God, the same is known of Him." This biography of Jabez stands in emphatic isolation upon the Sacred Page. Many of the persons in the genealogical list served under a national king, and verse 23 says that each "dwelt with the king for his work." But what a difference. *They* served *earthly* kings; *Jabez* served *Heaven's King*. Their names appear like those in a telephone directory, with no singular message. But the story and example of Jabez abide to bless the people of God until the end of time. So we would be wise to learn God's lessons from the exceptional portrait of Jabez included briefly in this too-regular list of names.

II. The Appeal of Jabez

Second, think of the *appeal* of Jabez. This text is universally labeled "the prayer of Jabez". There are 425 names listed in this long (*long!*) genealogical section—and Jabez is "only mentioned" because of a prayer! His name is highlighted because he prayed! So we have already discovered one of God's priorities for humanity. It is God's will that "men pray everywhere." In Luke 18:1, Jesus indicated that "men ought always to pray, and not to faint." Here, the foundational principles of prayer fairly shout from the page: (1) God hears prayers; (2) God answers prayers; but only (3) When the particular prayer agrees with His Purposes.

Tennyson was right when he said that "more things are wrought by prayer than this world dreams of." But the flip-side is also true—more follies are wrought due to "no-prayer" than this world dreams of! And there is a middle-ground problem as well. "You ask, and receive not, because you ask amiss, that you may consume the answer on your own lusts" (James 4:3). We may be sure that Jabez' prayer is not nickel-and-dime prayer. This is not a "trivia pursuit" prayer! And it certainly is not marked by the usual complacent selfishness manifested in many, if not *most*, prayers today.

The prayer of Jabez is highlighted in the text with the graphic words, "Jabez called on the God of Israel." His prayer is a *"calling upon God"*, not a merely formal prayer. One of the great puzzles of my mind during my years as a pastor was that many believers seem to have memorized a prayer, and they repeated essentially the same prayer every time they prayed aloud. Where is the Romance with God in that kind of prayer? The prayer of Jabez was not a lifeless recitation of rote religion, not a yawning "Now I lay me down to sleep" recitation of "vain repetition". Indeed, if it had been such, he surely would not have prayed as he did. There is a sense of urgency and earnestness presented by the word, "called", and it is evident that personal, passionate, persistent boldness was a major ingredient in the prayer. A man whose soul never "calls", never cries, never looks, never waits upon God, is not living to and for the purpose for which He was made. We need to recite our wants and our needs simply to remind our own minds and hearts of our utter helplessness and unworthiness.

Furthermore, the description of God as "the God of Israel" places Jabez' prayer *in the context of a covenant* between God and a chosen nation. Israel was not an ideal national Paradise, but the nation had graciously been brought into league with God at God's initiative. Jabez seemed to have appealed to God on the basis of this privilege and right. So he made *a claim upon God founded on God's own covenant with His own people*. We may also draw this further devotional thought from this story—in order to have an effective prayer *life*, each believer should form an intelligent and God-guided prayer *list. Jabez had a clear-cut prayer list!* If I am wise—*if I am wise*—I will ask God to purify my heart from self-intoxication and self-addiction, and then pray these concerns of Jabez, making them my God-centered prayer list for my daily life.

The prayer of Jabez looks like the personification of selfishness, but a little thought will disclose that this judgment is unfounded. The fact that God calls him "honorable" and that God heard and granted his request sets the prayer "outside the box" of selfish prayers. So what is the true and exact meaning of the requests of his prayer?

A. A Blessed Man

The entire appeal of Jabez reveals that he wants to be a *truly blessed* man. The words "truly" and "blessed" are determinative words in describing the request of his prayer. His prayer is laced with faith. "Oh, that You would...." shows his passion, poignancy and humility. Jabez first asks God to "bless me indeed." The word "me" makes the prayer sound selfish, but the word "bless" qualified by the word "indeed" allows God to determine the blessing received. Jabez not only wants to be a blessed man after the popular definition of blessedness, he wants to be a *God*-blessed man who defers to *God's own understanding* of true, spiritual, eternal blessedness! The word "indeed" indicates that he is willing to bypass his own selfish views of being blessed, and even the conventional view of being blessed that was usual among his Jewish contemporaries. If Jabez lived today, he would surely bypass the usual selfish prayers of the usual believer, and press into the purposes of God for his life.

The word "indeed" reveals that Jabez had recognized a difference between being blessed and being "indeed" blessed! The word "indeed" means really, actually, truly and fully—i. e., in the superlative and qualitative sense. Jabez knew the difference between the material blessings man seeks and the merciful blessings, spiritual blessings, eternity-oriented blessings, the strategy-fulfilling blessings, that God prioritizes—and he asked God for the latter blessings. Dear friend, have you realized that God wants to determine your dreams and desires, and then bless you accordingly?

The text prompts a serious question: Is ambition wrong for a Christian? Biblically, the answer is a decisive "NO!" but with a proviso added. Jesus said, "He that would be great among you…." (see Matthew 20:25-28). Greatness is not wrong for a Christian. Indeed, Jesus clearly offered it to His followers, but with a qualification. *God's* Greatness—the only true greatness there is—is determined by character, relationship, devotion and service built into the believer by God. Jesus would advise, "Just be sure that the greatness you seek is real greatness, defined by God and His purposes, not implemented by/through your sinful self-addiction." We must be God-determined in purpose, God-big in plans, God-centered in the execution of His plans, God-constructed in character, and God-defined and God-blessed in product, if we are to be "blessed indeed". I have re-read the previous sentence again and again, and my heart pursues God more and more with each new reading.

In a context that counsels us to "fret not because of evildoers", to "trust in the Lord", to "commit your way unto the Lord", to "rest in the Lord, and wait patiently for Him", David summarizes the entire contract in these incredible words: *"Delight yourself also in the Lord, and He shall give you the desires of your heart"* (Psalm 37:4; see the entire Psalm). Of course He will, because if you *truly delight in Him*, He forms, forges, and frames your prayer, and He will honor His own desires formed in your heart by granting them! God simply does not disagree with Himself! If He can ever draw us into such a relationship with Him that His desires are created in us through a heart that is so captivated by Him that it may be said to "delight in Him", the granting of the request is a foregone conclusion. In short, when we are brought into full agreement with Him and "deny ourselves" of fleshly desires, He Himself prays within us even with inarticulate groanings (Romans 8:26-28), and *God agrees with His own interests expressed in and through us!* May each of us pray today as Jabez prayed then, "Oh, that You would bless me indeed!"

B. A Bigger Man

Jabez' second appeal was that God would make him a *bigger* man—but only after God's true standard of bigness. Jabez prayed, "Enlarge my coasts." A coast is a boundary line, such as the dividing line between one territory and another, or such as forms the boundary of an island. The prayer of Jabez graphically expresses one of God's greatest purposes for each of His children. God wants each of His children to stop thinking small, acting small, contributing small, and being gratified by meager performance and production for Him. In short, He doesn't approve of the usual, conventional, survivor-oriented, non-productive life of the western Christian. He doesn't want His children defined by the sad littleness depicted in this line: "Edith is a lonely territory, bounded on the North, South, East and West—by Edith."

In his inaugural address as the first black President of South Africa, Nelson Mandela said to his fellow black South Africans, "Your playing small does not serve God." May the Holy Spirit register that sentence in the mind and heart of every reader of these words. No Christian should be satisfied with a feel-good, to-church-and-back, "faithful" routine, that shows no Book-of-Acts, "all nations" (Matthew 28:19, et al),"much fruit that remains" (John 15:16, et al), clout for God! No Christian should ever be satisfied with a merely church-centered smallness—and let no one think that I am depreciating the fellowship of believers and the role of each believer in it. But that implosive attitude toward a "meeting house" is not the Christianity initiated, exemplified and mandated by Jesus Christ. If that attitude defined Jesus, the Apostles and the early church, where is the evidence for it in the New Testament?

The typical "church-going" of today seems to be a misnomer, since *the people are the church, and the individual member is already "in the church" and functioning as the church wherever he goes.* Read carefully the story of Philip and the Ethiopian eunuch in Acts 8:26-39). The typical Christianity of the western church today is an example of "playing small." Please don't insist on misunderstanding me. I have spent my life as a "church-going" Christian, as the church often depicts it. But may God pity me if I ever make *that* the end of my Christian living, serving, contributing, and producing. No Christian fellowship I have ever attended—and I have attended some "great" ones—has stretched me (or anyone I know) to the Jesus-revealed, Jesus-intended, Jesus-declared level of fruitfulness and productivity.

Without explanation or apology, the Holy Spirit records that Jabez prayed, "Enlarge my coast". That is, "Enlarge my sphere of life and influence." The born-again person surely will earnestly desire to have his coast enlarged. "More light, more life, more liberty, more devotion, more knowledge of God in Christ, more faith, more hope, more love," will be the cry of his heart. Lord, enlarge the boundaries of my thinking, my planning, my action, my sphere of influence, my place of impact for You, my ministry in Your Name. Can we possibly believe that God would disapprove of that prayer, when we have vast multitudes of Christians who have shrunk these areas of their lives into a next-to-nothing smallness? Is it not a reality that multitudes of potential world-impacting individual Christians are hiding in the collective security of "the missions ministry of my church"—when *the assignment was given to individuals* who make up the church? Note again the individuality of Jabez' request. If the assignment of Christ was given to each individual, this makes up the total church. But if the assignment is given to the "active members", then "the church" simply cannot be mobilized. How in the world does a church whose "roll" is crowded with inactive and indifferent members, and with many of the "regulars" attending only at their leisure, think that *it* can impact the world according to the standard of Jesus? If we then say that it is the *active* people who must do it, have we not admitted my premise? All we must do to test this is to measure the performance of any church against the potential of its numbers. If every Christian just aspired to live, serve, contribute, impact, and penetrate outward, as the New Testament counsels and commands, *indeed, as Jesus declared and expects*, the outcome would be quite different. But again, we seem to be armored by a mentality that makes realism at this point an impossibility. True Spirit-led, God-piercing, self-assessment seems off limits to most fellowships of believers today—so we settle back to the mediocrity of the "norms". The basic problem seems to be that we refuse to even examine the disparity between New Testament Christianity and a church full of "convenience Christians". Question: are we not experiencing Satan's *curse of complacency* in many areas of our lives and the fellowship of our churches?

In a great miracle account in Luke 5, Jesus gave a strategy statement to His followers when He said, "Launch out into the deep and let down your nets." If the church operated just by the two "Ls" of that verse and held those as imperatives before each believer, what would happen? In the

Luke 5 text, both "L" words are *aorist active imperative* verbs, clearly calling for *a crucial and decisive attitude* (the aorist tense), *a lifestyle of crisis action* (the active voice), and *a sense of urgent obedience* (the imperative mood). In that story, Jesus clearly challenged His men to venture far beyond their previous endeavor ("launch out into the deep"), and to use maximum mobilized effort ("and let down your nets") to bring in *His intended* catch of fish. Does the story need more application here? Christian, do you have any idea of how far God wants to stretch you beyond your present "limits", and how He expects you to rearrange your life to accommodate His purpose for you? *Giving birth to something great requires much stretching!* I am impelled to say in His behalf that someone reading these words needs to *immediately secure a passport* in order to accommodate the "enlarged coasts" of this prayer.

    I want to quote a lengthy two verses found in the "Suffering Servant" section of Isaiah (chapters 40-66 is the section; I quote verses 5 and 6). I am writing under the assumption that this passage refers to Jesus, His Suffering Servant. "And now saith the Lord that formed me from the womb to be His servant, to bring Jacob again to him, Though Israel be not gathered, yet shall I be glorious in the eyes of the Lord, and my God shall be my strength. And He said, It is a light (marginal note, "small") thing that You should be My servant to raise up the tribes of Jacob and to restore the preserved of Israel: I will also give You for a light to the Gentiles, that You may be My salvation unto the end of the earth." Here, God seems to be extending the influence of Jesus far beyond the borders of His country, Israel, to all nations and all peoples. Though He was sent to "the lost sheep of the house of Israel", it is conspicuous to us today that, had Jesus only played by that "small map", most of us would never have received His Gift of Eternal Life. So God the Father even "enlarged the coasts" of His own Son's ministry! The Father said to His unique Son, "It is a small thing for You to merely be the Shepherd of Israel; You are to be the Good Shepherd for people from all nations."

I just read this note I made on someone else's sermon in a service years ago: "The great danger is not that you don't do what *others* do; the great danger is that you don't get near to what *you can/could do!*" Apparently, the goal of Jabez was progressive and steady growth into ever-enlarging new territory, and I am convinced that this is God's intention for each of His children as well. "O that you would expand my spiritual growth and my sphere of impact." I want to truly be a far, far bigger man with a true impact for You than I have ever been before. This prayer is an individual request for individual fulfillment, and does not even mention a corporate fulfillment, so I am perfectly satisfied that God will be pleased if I echo this prayer today—and expect its immediate fulfillment! Furthermore, if each believer regularly prayed, and implemented the answer to, this personal prayer, the church's influence and ministry would be extended abroad many times over its present impact—and this is true of even the "great" churches, as we label them.

C. A Bolder Man

Third, Jabez' prayer is a passionate request that God make him a *bolder* man. "And that Your Hand might be with me." At this point, one commentator says that the Hebrew word used here for "hand" means an *open* hand. In short, it seems to be a prayer to know the full provision, the full power, and the full guidance of God in his life. If this prayer is answered for me, I will know the precious touch of God upon my life. I will know God's "handling" of me and my concerns.

Evidently, Jabez asked for God's Hand to be with him because he was thoroughly persuaded that without the Lord he could do nothing. Dear friends, do we not need God's gracious and glorious touch on our persons, our attitudes, our schedules, our families, our marriages, our churches, our relationships, our witness, and our actions? In short, we need *God's total action in our total lives.* Without this, we can't live the Christian life, make the Christian commitment, fulfill the Christian vocation, see God's specified "all nations" product for our lives. The "with me" phrase in Jabez' prayer calls for the constant and attending Hand of God upon everything I am, say and do, as well as in every place of my assignment all over the world. Remember, this is an individual prayer and cannot be fulfilled by a corporate substitute. But we must also remember this rule: Sanctified ambitions such as those expressed in this prayer must be endowed with the sanctifying power of God. Thus, the appeal for His Hand to be with me. May God never pass the judgment upon me/you that we continue our activities and even engage in His work—but without His power. And may I be cleansed of anything that would dislodge His Hand from its proper place in my life.

Regarding the great early church in Antioch, Luke records these words in Acts 11:21, *"And the hand of the Lord was with them, and a great number believed, and returned to the Lord."* This is especially meaningful to me today in that I have just returned from a trip to Africa in which in one large city in Kenya I saw 600 young men in a public but elite boys' high school respond in a single service to the invitation to trust Christ and cooperate with His Purpose for their lives. First, I secured permission from the school administrators to preach the Gospel, and they seemed happy to allow it. I preached on the three descriptive adjectives Paul used in describing the will of God in Romans 12:2. Paul said that the will of God is "good, well-pleasing and complete." I clearly explained these three dimensions of the will of God for each person. Then I closed the message with a powerful illustration of the text, and God surely showed His pleasure over the entire event. It was obvious to me when I walked into the auditorium in which I was to speak, before I ever stood to preach, that the Hand of God was with me/us and that His endorsement would be upon this service. "Oh, God, keep Your Hand upon me/us/them! Make me a bolder and wiser man!"

D. A Better Man

Jabez' final request in his prayer was that God make him morally and spiritually a *better* man—purer, holier, spiritually cleaner—a truly sanctified man growing in the grace and knowledge of God and progressively purer in heart because of the Association. One translation says, "And that You would keep me from evil, that I might not experience the grief of sin or cause it for others." Here is a perfect example of the holy, wholesome, and realistic distrust of self that must characterize every serious child of God. What an incredible conclusion to a remarkable prayer!

Note in his request the connection between perversion and pain, between sin and suffering. Peter wrote (I Peter 3:18), "Christ has once suffered for sins." There is the inevitable connection! Suffering follows sin as day follows night, as your shadow follows your body when you stand in the sunshine. The curse of sin always yields the consequence of suffering. Jabez admitted, "If I yield to the practice of sin, I will receive the product of suffering." And this is not only a personal edict; I will *"cause* pain" to *others* if I allow the downward spiral of sin to prevail in my life. Up to this point, the Holy Spirit has recorded this prayer as an individual endeavor of this one man, Jabez, but at this point, the Holy

Spirit introduces into the record through his prayer the social dimension of our lives.

"That you would keep (guard, protect) me from evil." That is, guard me in times of temptation, in times of special arousings of the flesh, and from the evil influences of sin around me. Guard me from the recurrence of sin in me because of untamed flesh. Guard me from any and every malicious, malevolent work of Satan. Dear Christian, when you were first brought through God's salvation into peace with God, you instantly were brought into warfare with Satan. When God first said, "Receive My peace," Satan said to you, "I am now at war with you." Peace with God will always mean war with Satan. Jesus taught us to pray, not merely, "Forgive us our trespasses", but also, "Deliver us from evil and the Evil One."

Also, there is a suggestion here that great temptations and the possibility of great moral and spiritual failure come with great victories, great successes, great influence, great power—the very things Jabez is praying for. Jabez seemed to intuitively anticipate that with the increase of God's blessings, with the enlargement of spiritual opportunity, with increasing spiritual success in ministry, with new levels of commitment and challenge, Satan would increase his evil pressure on his life. Leonard Ravenhill often said as a 'rule of thumb' for a Christian that "when God opens the windows of Heaven to bless us, the devil will open the windows of Hell to blast us." Jabez knew this, so he wisely prayed for God to guard him and preserve him from sin.

In the King James Version of the Bible, the prayer of Jabez reads, "Keep me from evil, that it may not grieve me." Note the admission of Jabez that sin is always a grief. I remind you that Jabez' very birth was a cause of sorrow, pain and grief to his mother. She named him, "Jabez", which

The Daily Quiet Time

means "sorrow", or "pain", or "grief". Apparently, his mother unwittingly shadowed his entire future with the momentary sense of her pain probably experienced in childbirth. There is an Eastern adage which says, "When you were born, you wept, while all those around you rejoiced. So live, that when you die you may rejoice, while all those around you weep." Jabez had probably heard from his mother's lips the account of her special trauma and agony in his birth, and he tended to color his thoughts of himself by this part of his story. He had *caused* pain and grief to his *mother*, now he prays that God will prevent him causing a worse pain, a worse grief, to *others* by the possible weakness, willfulness and wickedness of fleshly failure in his life. What a practical application this prayer has in today's western church! Many have been the failures of Christians and Christian leaders. We require the mighty defense of the Almighty God, not only from the wiles of Satan, and the snares of the world that is "no friend of grace", but also from our very selves. We must passionately and persistently appeal to God to protect us. Remember that God had placed a hedge of protection around his servant Job, and that Satan couldn't touch him without Divine permission. We must magnify and count on God's hedge of protection around our moral and spiritual lives. "Oh, that You would guard us, protect us, keep us from evil, that we might not be a grief to ourselves or to others."

So here are the categories of Jabez' prayer list. He asks God for: (1) An enlarged *provision;* (2) An enlarged *province;* (3) An enlarged *power;* and (4) An enlarged *protection.* Now, just one final, delightful truth needs to be briefly mentioned.

III. The Approval of God

The text leaves us in no doubt of God's response to Jabez' prayer. We know it gained the *approval of God,* because the text simply states that "God granted him that which he requested." His package-prayer was fully answered! What a gratification to a believer's heart, to know that God hears and answers his personal prayers! But what should we expect? We are told that the Throne of God which we approach in prayer is a "throne of grace", and that we are urged to "come boldly" to it, and that we should know that we may "obtain mercy" (which suits our case as sinners) "and find grace to help in time of need" (which provides for all necessary resources, and even those required in times of deepest need). So, dear believer,

> "Let not conscience make you linger,
> Nor for fitness fondly dream,
> The only fitness He requires
> Is to feel your need of Him."

But I am not content to merely acknowledge the approval of God upon the life and character of Jabez. God has voted, and I want to cast my small ballot alongside His. I want to stand Jabez before my heart as my example, and I want to offer him to you as well. I want to make the prayers of Jabez a lifetime model for my praying. I had the privilege of reading the numerous testimonies of saints who had long before adopted the Jabez prayer as their model, and I was moved to see the difference between them and the "also-rans" around them. Every child of God alive on earth today has the same God to go to, and far greater light to guide you to Him, than Jabez had. We have incredible Gospel promises to encourage us. We have the Holy Spirit as our "stay-within Friend and Counselor." And most of all, we have a great Heavenly Advocate to sift, refine and present our prayer before a Loving Father. Move over, Jabez, and give me a moment's audience with the King. I assure you that your prayer will be heard again in Heaven today.

Do you ever wonder why the Holy Spirit, in writing for us a Book that will outlast the suns and stars of space, includes such long and monotonous lists of names such as the one in which our text occurs? In the full list, there are some 425 names included. Many readers would pass over such genealogical lists in the Bible. But pause a minute and think of this. *It is absolutely wonderful that we honor a God who likes to write names in His Book. Furthermore, it is wonderful to know that no one is unimportant to God.* God simply doesn't know any *"Whatsiznames"!* We have no information about most of the people named in such lists in the Bible, but God loves each of them and longs for each of them and wants each of them Home! At the very moment He blots out your sins through the effectiveness of the shed blood and atoning Death of Jesus, He also inscribes your name indelibly in the Lamb's Book of Life.

What is necessary for that moment to occur right now in your life? Admit honestly that you are a helpless and hopeless guilty sinner without Christ. Then confess your sins directly to Him. As you do so, remember that He infinitely loves you—not because you are loving, or lovely, or loveable, but because *He is love!* Remember, too, that He loved you enough to die for you personally, as if you were the only sinner who ever needed His Death. He tells you that "Today, when you hear His voice, (you must not) harden your heart." The Holy Spirit's voice sounds in your dead spirit, saying, "Just now, you must repent of your sins and open your heart, trusting Jesus, God's Dear Son, to come into your life, and receive Him into your heart by faith, and I will save you now and forever." That is the Voice that raises the dead! When you hear that Voice, the Holy Spirit quickens you to responsible action, and you must say "Yes" to Him. I pray that you will do that today—and then begin to pray the prayer of Jabez as a model prayer for your life.